The C++
Programmer's Handbook

Paul J. Lucas
AT&T

Bell Laboratories

Prentice Hall, Englewood Cliffs, New Jersey 07632

Library of Congress Cataloging-in-Publication Data

Lucas, Paul J.
    The C++ programmer's handbook / Paul J. Lucas.
        p.   cm.
    Includes bibliographical references and index.
    ISBN 0-13-118233-1
    1. C++ (Computer program language)   I. Title.
    QA76.73.C153L83   1992
    005.13'3--dc20   91-40969
                                                         CIP

Editorial/production supervision: *Harriet Tellem*
Cover design: *Bruce Kenselaar*
Prepress buyer: *Mary E. McCartney*
Manufacturing buyer: *Susan Brunke*
Acquisitions editor: *Gregory G. Doench*

Published by Prentice-Hall, Inc.
A Simon & Schuster Company
Englewood Cliffs, New Jersey 07632

The publisher offers discounts on this book when ordered in bulk quantities. For more information write: Special Sales/Professional Marketing, Prentice-Hall, Inc., Professional & Technical Reference Division, Englewood Cliffs, New Jersey 07632.

This handbook was typeset in Times-Roman, Helvetica, and Courier using an Apple Macintosh and Microsoft Word by the author. Proof pages were printed on a Kodak Ektaprint 1492 printer; final pages were printed on a AGFA Compugraphic CG9400 imagesetter.

Apple and Macintosh are registered trademarks of Apple Computer, Inc. Microsoft is a registered trademark of Microsoft Corporation.

Printed in the United States of America

10 9 8 7 6 5 4 3

ISBN 0-13-118233-1

Prentice-Hall International (UK) Limited, *London*
Prentice-Hall of Australia Pty. Limited, *Sydney*
Prentice-Hall Canada Inc., *Toronto*
Prentice-Hall Hispanoamericana, S.A., *Mexico*
Prentice-Hall of India Private Limited, *New Delhi*
Prentice-Hall of Japan, Inc., *Tokyo*
Simon & Schuster Asia Pte. Ltd., *Singapore*
Editora Prentice-Hall do Brasil, Ltda., *Rio de Janeiro*

Preface

This book was designed to be a handy reference allowing fast look-up of information on C++, the Preprocessor, and the Input/Output and other libraries for both the novice and experienced C++ user.

The aim of this book is to be a C++ "programmer's companion," sitting next to a computer or terminal allowing you to look up this or that without having to wade through long paragraphs looking for what you want.

Toward this end, the presentation of information is as follows:

Headings Like This...

• Start a new subject.

• May use an ellipsis ("...") to form the first few words of sentences completed by each item in the bullet-list that follows (in the same manner as this example is being presented now).

Headings Like This...

• Start a new topic for the current subject.

• May also use an ellipsis to form the first few words of sentences completed by each item in the bullet-list that follows.

This book does not attempt to teach C++ programming; however, techniques for using certain language features as well as subtle relationships between various features are presented.

Acknowledgments

Thanks to Bjarne Stroustrup for giving us C++ and answering a few questions. Thanks to Jim Coplien, Brad Euhus, Dennis Mancl, Warren Montgomery, Griff Smith, and the "external reviewers" for their comments on draft copies of this book; to Valerie Monroe for making me a beta tester and giving me a pre-release copy of the 3.0 release of C++ to test my 3.0-specific examples; and to Morris Bolsky for the original *C Programmer's Handbook* that served as the starting point for this book.

Naperville, Illinois　　　　　　　　　　　　　　　　　*Paul J. Lucas*

Bibliography

AT&T Unix System Laboratories: *Unix System V—USL C++ Language System: Product Reference Manual, Release Notes, and Selected Readings*, releases 2.0–3.0beta2, Unix Press, 1989–1991.

Morris I. Bolsky: *The C Programmer's Handbook*, Prentice Hall, New Jersey, 1985.

Margaret A. Ellis and Bjarne Stroustrup: *The Annotated C++ Reference Manual*, Addison-Wesley, Reading, Massachusetts, 1990.

Stanley B. Lippman: *C++ Primer*, Addison-Wesley, Reading, Massachusetts, 1989; second edition 1991.

Bjarne Stroustrup: *The C++ Programming Language*, Addison-Wesley, Reading, Massachusetts, 1986; second edition 1991.

Bjarne Stroustrup: *Parameterized Types for C++,* Journal of Object-Oriented Programming, Jan./Feb. 1988.

C++ Language

The C++ programming language is based on its predecessor C. Although much of the "C part" of C++ is unchanged, there are some differences. Additionally, C++ has undergone several changes since its initial release. Both differences from C and earlier releases of C++ are footnoted.

Comments...

- Begin with /*, end with */. These comments do not nest.

- Begin with //, end with newline[1]. Code containing these comments can be commented out by /* and */.

  Example:
  ```
  /* This is one big comment.
  for ( i = 0; i < 10; ++i ) // initialize vector
     a[ i ] = 0;
  */
  ```

- Are legal anywhere whitespace is.

Identifiers...

- Are a letter or underscore followed by letters, underscores, or digits[2].

  Examples: i, word_count, pi2

- Are case-sensitive, that is, foo is different from Foo.

- May be of any length[3].

---

[1] Don't use // comments on preprocessor lines (see "Comments" under "Preprocessor").

[2] Don't start your identifiers with an underscore or use a double underscore (__). Such identifiers are used by the C++ compiler for its own purposes.

[3] However, some implementations may impose a limit.

Keywords...

• Are reserved by the language (bold entries are new with C++):

asm	auto	break	case	**catch**
char	**class**	const	continue	default
delete	do	double	else	enum
extern	float	for	**friend**	goto
if	**inline**	int	long	**new**
operator	**overload**	**private**	**protected**	**public**
register	return	short	signed	sizeof
static	struct	switch	**template**	**this**
throw	**try**	typedef	union	unsigned
virtual	void	volatile	while	

The keywords catch, throw, and try deal with exception-handing which is not yet implemented in C++.

Initial releases of C++ use the overload keyword; it has become unnecessary. They also do not implement asm, private, protected, signed, template, nor volatile.

Some implementations also reserve the words fortran and pascal.

The keyword asm is not covered in this handbook since it is implementation-specific.

Constants

Signed Integer Constants...

- <u>Decimal</u>: Are an optional sign followed by a non-zero digit followed by any number of digits.

  Examples: 23, -42, +1991 `// + is legal, but not needed`

- Are of type `int` unless they exceed the largest representable signed integer that will fit into an `int` on the machine; in that case they are `long`.

Unsigned Integer Constants...

- Are non-negative integer or long integer constants.

- <u>Decimal</u>: Are designated by appending a `U` or a `u` to an integer or long integer constant.

  Examples: 23U, 42u, 1991UL

- <u>Octal</u>: Are a zero followed by any number of digits in the range 0–7.

  Examples: 027, 052, 03707

- <u>Hexadecimal</u>: Are a `0x` or `0X` followed by any number of digits or letters in the range a–f or A–F.

  Examples: 0x17, 0x2a, 0X7C7

- Are of type `unsigned int` unless they exceed the largest representable unsigned integer that will fit into an `unsigned int` on the machine; in that case they are `unsigned long`.

Long Integer Constants...

- Are signed or unsigned integer constants that have a greater magnitude than plain integer constants.

- Are explicitly designated by appending an `L` or an `l` (letter ell) to a signed or unsigned integer constant.

  Examples: 23L, 0x2aL, 1991ul

Floating-Point Constants...

- Have an integer part, a decimal point, a fractional part, an e or an E, and an exponent that can be signed.

- Can have either the integer or the fractional part omitted and either the decimal point or the exponent omitted.

  Examples: 3.14159, 3E8, 1., .2, 1.602e-19

- Are of type double unless they are followed by an F or an f in which case they are float or they are followed by an L or an l (letter ell) in which case they are long double.

  Examples:
  ```
  23F, 42f, 1991F          // floats
  3.14159L, 3E8L, 1.602e-19l   // long doubles
  ```

Character Constants...

- Are (most often) a single character surrounded by single quotes. These are of type `char`[1].

  Examples: `'m'`, `'7'`, `'+'`

- Have the numerical value of that character within the machine's character set.

  Example: `'A'` in the ASCII character set has the value 65.

- Use escape sequences to represent certain characters:

Null	NUL	`'\0'`
Alert (bell)	BEL	`'\a'`
Newline	NL (LF)	`'\n'`
Horizontal Tab	HT	`'\t'`
Vertical Tab	VT	`'\v'`
Backspace	BS	`'\b'`
Carriage Return	CR	`'\r'`
Formfeed	FF	`'\f'`
Backslash	\	`'\\'`
Single Quote	'	`'\''`
Bit Pattern[2]	0ddd	`'\ddd'`
Bit Pattern	0xddd	`'\xddd'`

- Can also be multiple characters surrounded by single quotes. These are of type `int`, but the actual value is implementation-dependent.

  Examples: `'ah'`, `'MPNT'`

---

[1] In C, character constants are of type `int`
[2] Allows a bit pattern to be described by one to three octal or hexadecimal digits.

String Constants...

- Are zero or more characters surrounded by double quotes.

  Examples: `"m"`, `"C++"`, `"No way, Jose!"`

- Have type `static char[]`, that is, a static vector of characters.

- Have the null character `\0` placed at the end by the compiler.

  Example:
  ```
  char five[] = "Five";   // five has 5 elements
  ```

- Use `\"` to include a quote within the string.

- Can span multiple lines if a `\` is the last character on a line; the `\` and the newline are discarded.

  Example:
  ```
  char *quote = "\"Diplomacy\" is letting them \
  have it your way."
  ```

- Are concatenated if adjacent[1].

  Example:
  ```
  // the two lines below amount to the same thing
  greeting1 = "Hello world!";
  greeting2 = "Hello " "world!";
  ```

Enumeration Constants...

- Are identifiers.

- Are a unique integral type[2]. (See "Enumerations" under "Declarations.")

---

[1] This has a use when using the preprocessor (see "Preprocessor").
[2] In C, enumerations are treated as being of type `int`.

Expressions...

- Are composed of one or more constants, variables, or function calls and zero or more operators.

  Examples: i = 0, C++, c = sqrt(a*a + b*b)

- Are considered true if they evaluate to be non-zero, false if zero.

Operators

The following shorthand will be used to describe operands:

e	Any expression.
v	Any expression that can receive a value.
i	integer or character
a	arithmetic (integer, character, or floating-point)
p	pointer
s	structure, union, or class
m	structure, union, or class member
f	function

These can be combined: *ie* for integer expression, as an example.

Arithmetic Operators

ae + *ae*	Sum.
pe + *ie*	Address *pe* + *ie* * sizeof(**pe*)[1].
ae - *ae*	Difference.
pe - *ie*	Address *pe* - *ie* * sizeof(**pe*).
pe - *pe*	Number of vector elements of type **pe* between[2].
-*ae*	Minus *ae*.
ae * *ae*	Product.
ae / *ae*	Quotient.
ie % *ie*	Remainder[3].

---

[1] If *pe* were to point into a vector of, say, double, *pe* + 1 would point to the next double, not the next byte, in memory.

[2] This is only valid if both *pes* point into the same vector. The result is of type ptrdiff_t defined in the standard header file <stddef.h>.

[3] The sign of the result is undefined if either or both *ies* are negative.

Logical Operators

$!e$ Negation.

$e_1 \parallel e_2$ Or. e_2 is evaluated only if e_1 is false.

e_1 && e_2 And. e_2 is evaluated only if e_1 is true.

Example:
```
if ( p && !*p ) // if p == 0, !*p is not evaluated
   *p = 1;
```

Relational Operators...

• Take either two arithmetic or pointer expressions[1].

== Equal to.

!= Not equal to.

< Less than.

<= Less than or equal to.

> Greater than.

>= Greater than or equal to.

Example:
```
inline int Inrange( int n, int lower, int upper ) {
   return lower <= n && n <= upper;
}
```

---

[1] For pointer expressions, the operators <, <=, >, and >= only make sense if both expressions relate to the same vector.

Assignment Operators...

$v = e$ Assign the value of e to v.

- Allow multiple assignments to be performed in the same statement where assignment proceeds from right to left.

Example: `a = b = c = 0;    // a = (b = (c = 0));`

- Can be combined with arithmetic or bitwise operators as in...

$$v\ operator=\ e$$

...which is shorthand for...

$$v = v\ operator\ (\ e\ )$$

...except that v is evaluated only once.

Examples: `i += j, x <<= 1`

Increment & Decrement Operators

iv++   Increment iv by 1; value is iv before.

++iv Increment iv by 1; value is iv after.

pv++   Increment pv by `sizeof( *pv )`; value is pv before.

++pv Increment pv by `sizeof( *pv )`; value is pv after.

`--`   (Same semantics as ++ but for decrement.)

Examples:
```
int i = 3, j, k;
j = i++;          // i = 4, j = 3
k = --j;          // j = 2, k = 2

char buf[3], *p = buf;
*p++ = 'a';       // buf[0] = 'a', p = &buf[1]
*++p = 'c';       // p = &buf[2], buf[2] = 'c'
```

Pointer & Vector Operators

&v	Address of *v*.
*pe	Contents addressed by *pe*.
*fpe	Function addressed by *fpe*. (See "Call" under "Functions.")
pe[*ie*]	Access element *ie* of vector *pe*. This is shorthand for * (*pe* + *ie*).

Example:
```
// these two functions are functionally equivalent
void VecCopy( char to[], const char from[] ) {
    for ( int i = 0; to[i] = from[i]; ++i );
}

// this one, however, uses more concise notation
void PtrCopy( char* to, const char* from ) {
    while( *to++ = *from++ );
}
```

Structure, Union, & Class Operators

sv.m	Data member of structure, union, or class.
spe->m	Shorthand for (**spe*) *.m*.
sv.mf	Member function of structure, union, or class.
spe->mf	Shorthand for (**spe*) *.mf*.
sv.*mp	Data member of structure, union, or class.
spe->*mp	Shorthand for (**spe*) *.*mp*
sv.*mfp	Member function of structure, union, or class.
spe->*mfp	Shorthand for (**spe*) *.*mfp*
s::m or *s::mf*	Qualify *m* or *mf* to structure, union, or class *s*.

Examples:
```
struct Point { int x, y; };
Point a, b, *pb = &b;
a.x = a.y = pb->x = pb->y = 1;

int Point::*coord = &Point::x;
a.*coord = pb->*coord = 2;      // a.x = b.x = 2
```

Bitwise Operators

$\sim ie$ One's complement.

$ie_1 << ie_2$ Left-shift ie_1 by ie_2 bits; vacated bits become zero.

$ie_1 >> ie_2$ Right-shift ie_1 by ie_2 bits; vacated bits become zero if ie_1 is unsigned, undefined if signed.

ie & ie And.

ie | ie Or.

ie ^ ie Exclusive or.

Examples:
```
char letterA = 'A';  // binary:  01000001
char letterB = 'b';          // 01100010
const char mask = 0x20;      // 00100000
char lower = letterA | 0x20; // 01100001
char upper = letterB & ~0x20; // 01000010
```

Miscellaneous Operators

$e_1 ? e_2 : e_3$ If e_1 is true, evaluate e_2, result is e_2; else e_3, result is e_3.

Example:
```
inline int Max(int a, int b) { return a>b ? a:b; }
```

e_1 , e_2 Evaluate e_1, then e_2; result is e_2.

Example:
```
void Reverse( int a[], int n ) {
    for ( int i = 0, j = n-1; i < j; ++i, --j ) {
        int t = a[i]; a[i] = a[j]; a[j] = t;
    }
}
```

$::v$ Access global variable v.

Example:
```
int count;               // global variable
// ...
void f() {
    int count = ::count;    // set local to global
    // ...
}
```

> sizeof *e*   Number of bytes for type of e^1.
>
> sizeof(*type*)   Number of bytes for type *type*.

Example:
```
char buf[ 100 ];
while ( cin.getline( buf, sizeof buf - 1 ) )
    cout << buf;
```

> *fe*(*e*, *e*, ...)   Call function with arguments (see "Call"
>   under "Functions").
>
> (*type*)*e*   Value of *e* converted to type $type^2$.
>
> *type*(e)   Value of *e* converted to type $type^3$.

Example:
```
char c, *cp = &c;
long cheat = (long)cp;   // obtain machine address
```

---

[1] The expression for the `sizeof` operator must be able to be evaluated at compile-time.

[2] In C++ and C jargon, this operation is called "typecasting" or just "casting."

[3] This alternate notation for typecasting is new with C++; however, it can only be used for "simple" types, that is those not containing pointer * or reference & notations. For example, `double(x)` can be used to convert x to double, but `int*(p)` can not be used to convert p to a pointer to int; `(int*)p` must be used instead.

Free Store Operators (new with C++)

new *type*	Allocate space for type *type* and return address[1]. For `class` types, a constructor is also called. If allocation fails, return zero.
new *type* [*ie*]	Allocate vector of type *type* having *ie* elements and return address. For `class` types, a constructor is called for each element.
delete *pe*	Deallocate space pointed to by *pe*[2]. For `class` types, a destructor is also called. If *pe* evaluates to zero, `delete` does nothing.
delete[] *pe*	Deallocate vector pointed to by *pe*[3]. For `class` types, a destructor is called for each element.

There exists a global variable `_new_handler` that is a pointer to a function taking no arguments and returning `void`; as is the case with all global variables, it is initialized to zero.

Whenever the `new` operator is unable to allocate memory, it checks `_new_handler`: if zero, it returns zero, otherwise the function pointed to is called.

Setting `_new_handler` to point to a function that reports the out-of-memory condition to the user and does some last-minute clean-up (such as saving a file to disk) is typical. Doing so relieves the user from checking the return-value of `new` for zero.

Example:
```
void MyNewHandler() {
    cerr << "OUT OF MEMORY, SORRY\n";
    // ...do some last-minute stuff here...
    exit( 1 );            // some non-zero code⁴
}

_new_handler = &MyNewHandler;
```

---

1 This outmodes the library function `malloc()` used in C.
2 This outmodes the library function `free()` used in C.
3 Initial releases of C++ require the number of elements in the vector to be supplied between the brackets.
4 See "`exit()`" under "`stdlib.h`" in the "Other Libraries" section.

Precedence & Associativity

Below, operators in higher groups have higher precedence; within a group, equal precedence.

Bold, italicized entries are right-associative; others are left-associative.

: :	***Global-scope-resolution***
: :	Class-scope-resolution
( )	Function-call
[ ]	Subscripting
. ->	Member-selection
sizeof	***Size***
!	***Logical-not***
~	***One's-complement***
- +	***Unary-minus, Unary-plus***
++ --	***Increment, Decrement***
& *	***Address, Dereference***
( )	***Type-cast***
new delete	Allocate, Deallocate
.* ->*	Member-selection through pointer
* / %	Multiply, Divide, Modulo (remainder)
+ -	Add, Subtract
<< >>	Left-shift, Right-shift
< <=	Less-than, Less-than-or-equal-to
> >=	Greater-than, Greater-than-or-equal-to
== !=	Equal-to, Not equal-to
&	Bitwise-and
^	Bitwise-exclusive-or
|	Bitwise-or
&&	Logical-and
||	Logical-or
?:	***Arithmetic-if***
=	***Assignment***
*= /= %= += -= <<= >>= &= ^= |=	
	Comma

Evaluation Order...

- Is mostly undefined by the language.

  Example: n = (a = x++) * (b = x++);

  Assuming x is 1 to start, if the evaluation of the * operands is left-associative, then a will be 1 and b will be 2; if the order is right-associative, then a will be 2 and b will be 1.

- Is *guaranteed* to be left-associative for the four operators: &&, ||, ?:, and , (comma).

Arithmetic Conversions

- If either operand is of type long double, double, or float, the other is converted to the same type, long double having the highest precedence[1].

- Otherwise, if an int can represent all the values of a char, unsigned char, short int, unsigned short int, enumerator, or enumeration type, then all such operands are converted to int; unsigned int otherwise[2].

- Then, if either operand is unsigned long, the other is converted to unsigned long.

- Otherwise, if one operand is long int and the other is unsigned int, and a long int can represent all the values of an unsigned int, then the unsigned int is converted to a long int; otherwise both operands are converted to unsigned long int[3].

- Otherwise, if either operand is long or unsigned, the other is converted to the same type, long having the higher precedence.

- Otherwise, both operands are int.

---

[1] In C, all floats are automatically promoted to double; in C++, this is no longer the case.

[2] In C, all signed operands are converted to int and all unsigned operands are converted to unsigned int no matter what.

[3] In C, all operands are converted to unsigned long int no matter what.

Statements

Expression Statements...

• Are expressions followed by a semicolon.

   Example: `language = C++;`

Labeled Statements...

• Are expression statements preceded by an identifier and a colon[1].

• May be the target of `goto` statements (see "`goto`").

   Example: `OUTTA_HERE: return result;`

Null Statements...

• Are simply a semicolon.

• Are used when no actual statement is needed following a label or a `while`, `do`, or `for` statement.

   Example: `while ( *p++ = *q++ ) ;`

Compound Statements...

• Are zero or more statements enclosed by braces `{ }`.

• Are legal anywhere an expression statement is legal.

• Define a new scope, that is, variables declared inside are local to them and hide variables outside with the same name.

   Example: `{ int t = a; a = b; b = t; }`

• Have the destructor for local variables of a class, if any, called upon exit from them, however accomplished[2]. (See "Destructors" under "Classes.")

---

1   Label identifiers are distinct from all other identifiers and are local to the functions in which they are used.

2   In addition to "just falling out the bottom," `goto`, `break`, `continue`, and `return` statements can cause a compound statement to be exited.

Declaration Statements...

• Introduce an identifier and its type[1]. (See "Declarations.")

break;

• Terminates execution of the smallest enclosing while, do, for, or switch statement.

• Continues execution following the terminated statement.

Example:
```
for ( int i = 0; i < 10; ++i )
   if ( guess == a[i] ) {
      cout << "Congratulations!\n";
      break;              // this terminates the for
   }
if ( i == 10 )            // execution continues here
   cout << "Sorry\n";
```

continue;

• Continues execution at the bottom of the smallest enclosing while, do, or for statement; equivalent to a goto bottom in any of what's below:

```
while (...) {      do {                  for (...) {
   // ...             // ...                // ...
   goto bottom;       goto bottom;          goto bottom;
   // ...             // ...                // ...
   bottom: ;          bottom: ;             bottom: ;
}                  } while (...);         }
```

Example:
```
for ( int i = 0; i < 10; ++i ) {
   if ( a[i] == 0 )
      continue;        // don't do anything else
   // ...skip all this stuff this time around...
}
```

---

1 In C, all declaration statements have to precede all expression statements; this restriction has been lifted in C++.

`return` *expression*;

- Terminates execution of the current function and returns the value of *expression* to its caller. The *expression* is omitted if the function's return-type is `void`.

- Casts *expression* to the return-type of the current function if necessary.

`goto` *label*;

- Continues execution at the statement preceded by the given label (which must be within the current function).

  Example: `goto JAIL;`

- Can not skip over a declaration statement with an initializer at the same scope.

- Can not jump into a compound statement past a declaration statement with an initializer[1].

- Can jump out of a compound statement.

  Example:
  ```
  void Contrived() {
      goto L1;        // error...
      int a = 0;      // ...can't skip past this line
  L1:
      goto L2;        // ok...
      int b;          // ...not initialized
  L2:
      goto L3;        // ok, but dubious
      goto L4;        // error...
      for (;;) {
          int c;
      L3:
          int d = 0;  // ...can't skip past this line
      L4:
          goto L5;    // can leave a compound statement
      }
  L5:
      ;
  }
  ```

---

[1] This is legal in C, however.

`if (` *expression* `) statement`[1] `else statement`[2]

- Evaluates *expression* and if it is true, executes *statement*[1], otherwise *statement*[2][1].

- Can have the `else` and *statement*[2] omitted.

```
switch ( expression )          // first form (rare)
   case constant-expression₁:
   case constant-expression₂:
   ...
      statement
```

```
switch ( expression ) {        // second form (common)
   case constant-expression₁:
   case constant-expression₂:
   ...
      statements
   case constant-expression₃:
   case constant-expression₄:
   ...
      statements
   default:
      statements
}
```

- In its first form (which is rarely used), it's shorthand for...

```
if ( expression == constant-expression₁
   || expression == constant-expression₂
   ...
) statement
```

...except that *expression* is evaluated only once.

Example:
```
switch ( n )
   case 2: case 4: case 6: case 8:
      appreciate = n;
```

---

1 Neither *statement* can be a declaration statement, although they can be compound statements that contain declaration statements.

- In its second form, evaluates *expression* and executes the series of *statements* following the matching *constant-expression,* otherwise executes the series of *statements* following the `default` case[1].

- Note that execution will not stop at the end of a `case` (this allows multiple cases to execute the same series of statements); most of the time, a `break` statement is needed to exit the `switch`.

  Example:
  ```
  switch ( c ) {
     case '+': n = a + b; break;
     case '-': n = a - b; break;
     case '*': n = a * b; break;
     case '/': n = a / b; break;
     default:
        Error( "Bad operator: ", c );
  }
  // execution continues down here after any break
  ```

- Must have all *constant-expressions* unique.

while (*expression*) *statement*

- Is shorthand for...

  ```
  label:   if ( expression ) {
               statement
               goto label;
           }
  ```

do *statement* while (*expression*);

- Is shorthand for...

  ```
  label:   statement
           if ( expression ) goto label;
  ```

---

[1] The `default` case is optional; additionally, it need not be last.

```
for ( statement₁ expression₁; expression₂ )
    statement₂¹
```

- Is shorthand for...

  statement₁
  ```
  while ( expression₁ ) {
  ```
      statement₂
      expression₂;
  ```
  }
  ```

  ...except that a `continue` in *statement₂* will continue execution
  at *expression₂*.

- If *statement₁* is a declaration², the scope of the variables declared
  extends to the end of the compound statement enclosing the `for`
  statement.

- Can have *statement₁* null and both expressions omitted (but both
  semicolons must remain). When *expression₁* is omitted, it is
  taken to be non-zero.

Program Organization

C++ programs generally consist of two classes of files: header files
and code files. Header files typically end with a `.h` and code files
end with a `.c`. There are usually several of each type for any non-
trivial program.

Header files contain class, template, structure, union, enumeration,
and function declarations; `typedef`s, constant definitions, inline
functions, and preprocessor directives. These make up the
interface of code files; code files contain the *implementations*.

---

1 Note that *statement₁* is a *statement*, meaning that it ends with a semicolon.
2 In C, *statement₁* can only be an expression.

Declarations...

- Introduce a new type, a variable and its type, a constant and its value, or a function, its arguments, and its return-value type.

- Are assumed to be of type `int` if no type is explicitly specified.

Static & Automatic Storage Class

All variables declared outside of a function have *static storage class*, that is they exist for as long as the *program* is executing[1]; all variables, declared inside of a function have *automatic storage class* by default, that is, they exist only as long as the *function* is executing.

To make a variable declared within a function have static storage class, prefix the declaration with the `static` keyword[2].

> *Example*:
> ```
> void Dryer( int clothes ) {
>     static cling;     // lasts as long as program
>     // ...
> }
> ```

By default, `static` variables are initialized to zero (or equivalent) before they are used and before any run-time initializations (those that involve expressions). Automatic variables are not initialized.

---

[1] These are commonly referred to as "global" variables.
[2] Automatic variables may be preceded by the `auto` keyword; it has no use other than to serve as a readability aid.

Static & External Scope

Static storage class variables declared outside of functions normally have external scope, that is, the variables in one file can ordinarily be accessed in another file by prefixing the declaration with the `extern` keyword.

Example:
```
// file 1
int global;

// file 2
extern int global;    // accesses file 1's global
```

To make a static storage class variable declared outside of a function inaccessible to other files, prefix the declaration by the `static` keyword[1]. The `static` keyword changes the scope of the variable from external scope to file scope[2].

Example:
```
// file 1
static electricity;        // local to file 1

// file 2
extern electricity;        // link-time error

// file 2a
int electricity;           // ok: distinct
```

Since `electricity` in file 1 is restricted to that file, a different `electricity` can be declared in any other file.

---

[1] Functions may also be declared `static` for the same reason; however, the same effect may be achieved by not placing the declaration in a header file since all functions must be declared before use in C++. This ability is for compatibility with C only.

[2] The `static` keyword has changed its meaning from "permanent" to "private" in this context.

Simple Types...

- Are any of the following:

`char`	Character (one byte).
`unsigned char`	Unsigned character.
`signed char`	Signed character.
`int`	Integer (typically, one word).
`unsigned int`	Non-negative integer (has `int` size).
`short int`	Small integer (word or half-word).
`unsigned short int`	Non-negative, small integer.
`long int`	Large integer (word or double-word)[1].
`unsigned long int`	Non-negative, large integer.
`float`	Single-precision floating-point.
`double`	Double-precision floating-point.
`long double`	High-precision floating-point.
`void`	No value[2].

By themselves, `unsigned`, `short`, and `long` are equivalent to `unsigned int`, `short int`, and `long int`, respectively. By itself, `char` is `signed` or `unsigned` depending on the compiler.

All that is guaranteed about integer sizes is that...

$$\text{sizeof(short)} \leq \text{sizeof(int)} \leq \text{sizeof(long)}$$

...although `long` is usually twice the size of `short` in a given implementation. All that is guaranteed about floating-point sizes is that...

$$\text{sizeof(float)} \leq \text{sizeof(double)}$$
$$\leq \text{sizeof(long double)}$$

- Can be initialized by an expression.

Examples:
```
char broiled;
unsigned check = 197;
long distance = AT&T;
```

---

[1] Some implementations may have a `long long` type for very large integers (quad-word).

[2] No `void` objects can be declared; however, pointers to `void` can (see "Pointers"). Also, functions can have a return-type of `void` to indicate that they return no value (see "Functions").

Enumerations...

- Allow meaningful names to be used instead of numeric values.

- Can be given a name that becomes a type.

- Can be assigned specific (integer) values; subsequent values progress from that value. (If no values are given, they progress from zero.) Multiple enumerations can have the same value.

Examples:
```
enum { chocolate, vanilla, strawberry };
// chocolate = 0, vanilla = 1, strawberry = 2

enum Fruit { orange, cherry, banana }; // a type

enum Cost { perPerson = 2, perCouple /* = 3 */ };

Fruit florida = orange; // declare Fruit variable[1]
```

- Must be distinct in the same scope.

Example:
```
enum State { start, run, stop };
enum Position { start, middle, end };  // error
```

- Can be declared within a class (see "Classes"). These are local to the scope of the class[2].

Example:
```
class IceCream {
    // ...
public:
    enum Flavor { chocolate, vanilla, strawberry };
    Flavor flavor;
    // ...
};
// ...
    Flavor favorite;  // error: Flavor not in scope
    IceCream homeMade;
    homeMade.flavor = chocolate;             // error
    homeMade.flavor = IceCream::chocolate; // ok
```

---

[1] To declare an enumeration variable in C, the enum keyword has to be used explicitly (unless typedef is employed); in C++, the enum keyword is no longer required although it is still permitted (for compatibility).

[2] In earlier releases of C++, enumerations are not local to a class's scope.

Vectors...

- Are contiguous blocks of memory for storage of the same type.

- Are declared by specifying the number of elements, which must be a constant positive integral expression, between brackets [ ].

- Have only one dimension. Multidimensional arrays found in other languages are represented in C++ by a vector of pointers to vector.

Examples:
```
float vf[10];      // vector of 10 float
int vvi[50][8];    // 50 vectors of vector of 8 int
char *vpc[5];      // vector of 5 pointers to char
```

- Can be initialized (if they have static storage class); values are listed between braces { }. Vectors of char are a special case and can be initialized with a string constant.

The left-most number of elements can be omitted in which case it equals the number of values. If the number of elements is given and the number of values is less than that, then the remaining elements are initialized to zero (or equivalent). If all the values for a size are given, then that set of braces can be omitted.

Examples:
```
char greeting[] = "Yes, master?";   // 13 elements¹

int a[5] = { 7, 6, 9 };             // a[3] = a[4] = 0

int b[][2] = { {1, 2}, {3, 4}, {5, 6} };  // [3][2]

int c[][2] = { 1, 2, 3, 4, 5, 6 };     // omit { }
int d[][2] = { {1}, {3}, {5} };  // can't omit { }
// d[0][1] = d[1][1] = d[2][1] = 0
```

The name of a vector by itself evaluates to the address of its first element:

$$v \equiv \&v[0]$$

The only exception is when the name of a vector is used with the sizeof operator: sizeof v refers to the number of bytes in the entire vector, not just the first element.

---

[1] Remember, the compiler places a null character at the end of string constants.

Pointers...

- Are variables that contain the address of a variable or function. (See also "Pointers to Members" under "Classes.")

- Are declared using the * character.

  Examples:
  ```
  int i, *pi = &i;   // pointer to int
  int **ppi = &pi;   // pointer to pointer to int
  char (*pvc)[5];    // pointer to vector of 5 char
  float (*pf)(int);  // pointer to function taking
                     // one int and returning float
  ```

- Provide a mechanism for a function to change the value of its arguments[1].

  Example:
  ```
  inline void Swap( int* a, int* b ) {
      int t = *a; *a = *b; *b = t;
  }
  // ...
      Swap( &x, &y );        // must pass addresses
  ```

- Can be of type "pointer to void" which means that they can point to any non-const or non-volatile object. The conversion of a pointer to a void pointer is implicit; a type cast is required to convert a void pointer back to a pointer to a real object[2].

  Example:
  ```
  char c, *p = &c;
  void *v = p;           // implicit conversion
  char *q = (char*)v;    // explicit cast required
  ```

---

1 In C, this is the only way to change the value of arguments; C++ offers references (see "References").
2 In C, no type cast is required.

References...

- Are aliases for other variables.

- Are declared using the & character.

- Must be initialized in the declaration. (Once initialized, there is no way to change what a reference refers to.)

  Example:
  ```
  double agent = .028;
  double &bond = agent;    // bond refers to agent
  // ...
  bond /= 4.0;             // agent == .007
  ```

- May improve efficiency when passing large objects to functions since they won't be copied onto the stack[1].

  Example:
  ```
  // String is a class defined in <String.h>

  char LastChar( const String& s ) {
      return s.length() ? s[ s.length() - 1 ] : '\0';
  }
  // ...
      String word = "barbecue";
      char c = LastChar( word );
  ```

- Provide a mechanism for a function to change the value of its arguments.

  Example:
  ```
  inline void Swap( int& a, int& b ) {
      int t = a; a = b; b = t;       // no *'s or &'s
  }
  // ...
      Swap( x, y );   // no need to pass addresses
  ```

- Are mostly used when defining functions for class types.

---

[1] When using references solely to improve efficiency and not to change the value of arguments, it is preferred that the reference be declared const thereby enlisting the compiler's help in guaranteeing that the reference will not be changed and also assuring the user that it won't be.

- Are not a type unto themselves since, after initialization, no operation can be performed on a reference, only to the object to which it refers.

- Can not refer to other references nor bit fields (see "Structures"), nor can there be vectors of or pointers to references[1].

Constants...

- Are objects whose value may not be changed after initialization (which must be done when declared)[2].

  Examples:
  ```
  const long double pi = 3.14159265358979323846;
  const int prime[] = { 1, 2, 3, 5, 7, 11 };
  ```

- For global constants, have file scope by default; to establish external scope, prefix the declaration by the `extern` keyword[3].

  Example:
  ```
  extern const int prime[] = { 1, 2, 3, 5, 7, 11 };
  ```

- Have two entities involved when pointers are used: the pointer and the object pointed to. Either, or both, can be constant.

  Examples:
  ```
  char a, b;

  const char *pcc = &a;    // pointer to const char
  pcc = &b;                // ok
  *pcc = 'Z';              // error

  char *const cpc = &a;    // const pointer to char
  cpc = &b;                // error
  *cpc = 'Z';              // ok

  const char *const cpcc = &a;   // both constant
  cpcc = &b;                     // error
  *cpcc = 'Z';                   // error
  ```

---

1   Although there can be references to pointers. For example, `int *&rpi` says that `rpi` is a reference to a pointer to an `int`.
2   Constants eliminate a use for the `#define` preprocessor directive as it is used in C.
3   In ANSI C, global constants have external scope by default.

Register Variables...

• May improve the speed at which automatic variables are accessed[1].

• Are designated by prefixing a declaration with the `register` keyword.

  Example: `register int i, *pint;`

• Can hold any data type that will fit into a machine register; for types that won't, the `register` specification is ignored.

• Are a small, limited resource. There is no guarantee that a variable declared as `register` will be placed into one; if not, the `register` specification is ignored.

• Can have the `&` operator applied to them (unlike C), but this will force the `register` specification to be ignored.

Volatile Variables...

• Are typically used to limit compiler optimization of variables whose contents may change due to external events[2].

  Example:
```
// serialPort is a memory-mapped I/O address
volatile char *const serialPort = (char*)0xA400;

char c = *serialPort;    // read serial port
c = *serialPort;         // read again (we mean it)
```

Without the `volatile` declaration, an optimizing compiler may eliminate the second assignment to `c` since, from its point of view, `*serialPort` could not have changed.

---

[1] Explicitly declaring variables as `register` is becoming unnecessary, if it isn't so already. Many compilers today are smart enough to determine for themselves which variables are heavily used and would benefit from being placed into registers. The `register` specification is therefore little more than a "hint" to the compiler as to which variables those are; the compiler is free to ignore the hint.

[2] The use and exact behavior of `volatile` variables is implementation dependent. Some implementations may not support `volatile` variables.

Structures...

- Are collections of related information, possibly of several types, combined into one object.

- Can be given a name; if so, it becomes a type[1].

  Example:
  ```
  struct Call {
      short area, exchange, line;
      enum { direct, oper_assist } type;
      enum { day, evening, weekend } rate;
  };
  // ...
  Call collect;           // declare Call variable[2]
  ```

- Can be initialized (if they have static storage class); values are listed between braces { } and are assigned in the same order as declared. Unspecified trailing values are initialized to zero (or equivalent).

  Example[3]:
  ```
  Call work = { 708, 555, 8887 };
  // work.type = direct, work.rate = day
  ```

  Static vectors of structures can also be initialized. If the number of values equals the number of structure members, then the inner sets of braces can be omitted.

  Example:
  ```
  Call record[] = {          // type = direct,
      { 516, 555, 8858 },    // rate = day
      { 508, 555, 0516 },    // for first two elements
      // can omit inner braces if all is specified
      212, 555, 5444, Call::direct, Call::weekend,
      908, 555, 6012, Call::oper_assist, Call::day
  };
  ```

---

1   The ability to omit a name is for backward compatibility with C.
2   To declare a structure variable in C, the `struct` keyword has to be used explicitly (unless `typedef` is employed); in C++, the `struct` keyword is no longer required although it is still permitted (for compatibility).
3   The example declaration is global.

- Can have *bit fields*. A bit field is a fraction of an integral type[1]. Uses for bit fields are that it saves data space[2], or that it allows data to conform to an external format[3].

  Unnamed bit fields serve as place-holders for the specified number of bits. An unnamed bit field with a size of zero specifies that the next bit field is to start on a word boundary.

  Example:
  ```
  struct Features {
      unsigned touchTone : 1;
      unsigned callWait : 1;
      unsigned callFwd : 1;
      unsigned threeWay : 1;
      unsigned : 2;                    // unused
      unsigned speedDial : 1;
      unsigned dstnctRng : 1;
  };
  ```

---

1   Whether an `int` in this context is `signed` or `unsigned` is implementation-dependent. To ensure getting the one you want, specify `signed` or `unsigned`. ANSI C only allows bit fields to be `int` (plain, `signed`, or `unsigned`); C++ allows any integral type.
2   At the expense of code space and performance.
3   However, the order that bit fields are stored within a machine word is implementation-dependent.

Unions...

- Are any *one* of several types combined into one object.

- Can be given a name; if so, it becomes a type.

- Have a size sufficient to store the largest member.

Example:
```
union Labor {
    int UAW;
    char teamsters;
    char* CWA;
};
// ...
Labor day;              // declare Labor variable[1]
```

- Can be initialized (if they have static storage class); values are listed between braces { }. Only the first member declared can be initialized.

Example[2]:
```
Labor day = { 5 };            // ok: 5 is an int
Labor intensive = { 'a' };    // error
```

Static vectors of unions can also be initialized.

Example:
```
Labor record[] = { 3, 4, 5 };
```

- Can be anonymous, that is, without a name[3]. Members are referred to as though they were not in a union[4].

Example:
```
union {
    long   jekyll[100];
    char*  hyde[100];
};

hyde[0] = "Dr. Jekyll";     // affects jekyll[0]
```

---

1 To declare a union variable in C, the union keyword has to be used explicitly (unless typedef is employed); in C++, the union keyword is no longer required although it is still permitted (for compatibility).
2 The example declarations are global.
3 Anonymous unions are new with C++.
4 Global anonymous unions must be declared static.

Type Aliasing...

- Introduces an identifier as a synonym for an existing type providing a more meaningful name or a shorthand.

- Is done by placing a "variable declaration" after the typedef keyword. Instead of declaring a variable of the given type, however, a synonym for that type is declared.

   Examples:
   ```
   typedef float GIGAWATT;
   typedef const char CHAR;
   // ...
   GIGAWATT future = 1.21;

   int MyFunction( char );

   // pointer to function taking char returning int
   typedef int (*PFCRI)( char );
   // ...
   PFCRI myFunctionPtr = &MyFunction;
   ```

- Can be done within a class (see "Classes"). The aliased type names are local to the scope of the class.

   Example:
   ```
   class C {
       // ...
   public:
       // pointer to member function of C
       // taking and returning an int
       typedef int (C::*PMFCIRI)( int );
       // ...
   };
   // ...
   PMFCIRI p;        // error: PMFCIRI not in scope
   C::PMFCIRI q;     // ok
   ```

Functions...

- Are collections of zero or more statements combined into an executable unit that performs a specific, user-defined operation.

- Are called by other functions and generally return a value to them (unless the function's return-type is `void`).

- Have a few varieties: regular (described here), member (see "Member Functions" under "Classes"), friend (see "Friend Functions" under "Classes"), and template (see "Templates").

Declaration...

- Specifies a function's name[1], return-type, and argument types[2].

  Example:
  ```
  // two double arguments and returns double
  double Hypotenuse( double a, double b );
  ```

- Can have argument names omitted[3].

  Example:
  ```
  // same as before from the compiler's point of view
  double Hypotenuse( double, double );
  ```

- Can specify default values for trailing arguments.

  Example:
  ```
  // optional char argument, '-' is the default,
  // and returns no value
  void PrintLine( int length, char = '-' );
  ```

---

1 In C++, all functions must be declared before they are used.
2 In ANSI C, `f()` means that the function takes zero or more arguments of an unspecified type; in C++, it means that the function takes no arguments. Both accept `f(void)` to mean that function takes no arguments.
3 However, their presence documents the function for the user.

- Can be *overloaded*, that is, more than one function may have the same name so long as each differs in the number or type of *non-default* arguments[1].

  Examples:
  ```
  // two double or two int arguments and returns
  // either double or int, respectively
  double Max( double, double );
  int Max( int, int );              // ok: overloaded

  // one int argument and a default argument,
  // but this is an error
  int Fluff( int, char = '*' );
  int Fluff( int, int = 0 );        // error
  ```

- Can include the ellipsis . . . argument that tells the compiler that zero or more arguments of an unspecified type are to follow[2].

  Example:
  ```
  void printf( const char* format ... );
  ```

---

1 For any type T, a T, a T&, a const T, and a volatile T are indistinguishable when arguments are passed; therefore, these alone can not be used to distinguish overloaded functions, nor can a function's return-type alone be used. However, a const T& and a const T* are distinguishable from a T& and a T*, respectively.

2 See "stdarg.h" under "Other Libraries" for implementing functions with a varying number of arguments of an unspecified type.

Definition...

- Supplies the code that is executed for a function when it is called.

- Can be declared `inline` to optimize very small functions[1].
  There is no guarantee that a function declared `inline` will be
  made so[2].

- Can have its arguments declared `register`.

- Must include at least one `return` statement for functions whose
  return-type is not `void`.

  Examples:
  ```
  inline double Hypotenuse( double a, double b ) {
     return sqrt( a * a + b * b );
  }

  void PrintLine( register char ch ) {
     for ( register int i = 0; i < 80; ++i )
        cout << ch;
     cout << endl;
  }

  inline double Max( double a, double b ) {
     return a > b ? a : b;
  }

  inline int Max( int a, int b ) {
     return a > b ? a : b;
  }
  ```

- Can have unnamed arguments. This can be done to reserve a
  place in an argument list for future considerations.

  Example:
  ```
  void Peek( unsigned int* p, int ) {
     cout << '*' << p << " = " << *p << '\n';
  }
  ```

---

1   Unlike ordinary functions, the code for `inline` functions is placed into
    header files. Inline functions mostly outmode a use for the `#define`
    preprocessor directive as it is used in C.

2   The reasons why not vary among implementations.

Call...

- Executes the code associated with a function.

- Is done directly, by name, or indirectly, through a pointer.

  Examples:
  ```
  c = Hypotenuse( a, b );              // directly
  int (*pfii)( int, int ) = &Max;
  int x, y;
  // ...
  int m = (*pfii)( x, y );             // via pointer[1]
  ```

- Has all arguments passed by value, that is, they are evaluated and copied onto the stack. Two exceptions:

  If an argument is a vector, then only the address of its first element is passed[2].

  If an argument is declared to be a reference, then the value is passed by reference, that is, it is evaluated and its address is placed onto the stack.

---

[1]   In the example, the compiler knows to set `pfii` to point to the `int` version of Max since `pfii` is of type "pointer to function taking two `int` arguments and returning `int`."

[2]   Actually, this isn't an exception since the name of a vector evaluates to the address of its first element (see "Vectors" under "Declarations").

`main()` *Function...*

- Is required by all C++ programs.

- Is the function in which program execution begins.

- Has one of two argument forms:

```
int main() { /* ... */ }
int main( int argc, char* argv[] ) { /* ... */ }
```

The latter is used to accept arguments from the environment in which the program is executed: `argc` is the argument count and `argv[]` is a vector of `char` pointers each pointing to an argument. `argv[0]` is the name used to execute the program and `argv[1]` to `argv[argc-1]` are the actual arguments.

Example[1]:
```
$ magic hat wand
```

argc	argv[0]	argv[1]	argv[2]
= 3	= magic	= hat	= wand

- Typically returns a status code to the program's environment using a `return` statement. (See "`exit()`" under "`stdlib.h`" in the "Other Libraries" section.)

- Can not be overloaded, have default arguments, called by the user, have its address taken, nor be declared `inline` or `static`[2].

---

[1] This example assumes some command-line interface where the command shown would be entered on the keyboard. The $ is the system prompt.

[2] In C, `main()` can be called by the user and have its address taken.

Linkage to C...

- Allows previously compiled C functions in other files to be called from C++ programs[1].

- Is done by declaring the C functions to be `extern "C"` in either of the two forms shown below[2]:

Examples:
```
// declare one C function
extern "C" int system( const char* );

extern "C" {        // declare several C functions
    long      atol( const char* );
    int       atoi( const char* );
    double    atof( const char* );
}
```

For the standard C header files, these `extern "C"` declarations are normally done for you; you would probably only have to do this sort of thing if you wanted to use some of your own C functions in your C++ programs.

---

1 The C++ compiler encodes function names to include the types of their arguments (among other things) to ensure that functions are called properly. Normally, this is of no consequence; however, to use C functions in a C++ program, the compiler must be told not to encode their names, otherwise the program would not link with the C object files.

2 Initial releases of C++ do not support this mechanism.

Classes...

- Provide a means for creating a wholly new type that can be integrated into the language.

- Are collections of related information, possibly of several types (data members), combined into one object along with methods for manipulating the stored data (member functions).

Declaration...

- Introduces a new type.

- Establishes access permissions of `private`, `protected`, or `public` for members. Unless specified, `private` is assumed.

  <u>Private</u> members can only be accessed by member and `friend` functions of the class (see "Friend Functions").

  <u>Protected</u> members can also be accessed by member and `friend` functions of derived classes[1] (see "Derived Classes").

  <u>Public</u> members can be accessed by anything.

- Is similar to declaring a `struct` (see "Structures" under "Declarations").

  Example:
  ```
  class Phone {
      int area, exchange, line;      // private
  protected:
      enum HookState { onHook, offHook } handset;
  public:
      Phone( int a, int e, int l ) {
          area = a, exchange = e, line = l;
          handset = onHook;
      }
      int OffHook() const { return handset==offHook; }
      void GiveDialTone();
      long AcceptDigits();
      void Ring() const;
  };

  // declare class variable
  Phone home( 516,555,8858 );
  ```

---

1 Initial releases of C++ do not have `protected` members.

- Can contain other `class` declarations. Nested classes are local to and in the scope of the enclosing class[1], but receive no special access permissions from nor give any to it.

  Example:
  ```
  class OuterShell {
      int oa;
  public:
      int ob;
      class InnerSelf {
          int ia;
      public:
          int ib;
          void Vague( OuterShell& o, int n ) {
              oa = n;          // error: which oa?
              o.oa = n;        // error: oa is private
              o.ob = n;        // ok: ob is public
          }
          void Later();        // defined outside
      };
      void Vague( InnerSelf& i, int n ) {
          ia = n;              // error: which ia?
          i.ia = n;            // error: ia is private
          i.ib = n;            // ok: ib is public
      }
  };

  InnerSelf shallow;           // error: not in scope
  OuterShell::InnerSelf deep;  // ok

  // how to declare an InnerSelf member function
  void OuterShell::InnerSelf::Later() { /* ... */ }
  ```

- Can contain local enumerations and `typedef`s (see "Enumerations" and "Type Aliasing" under "Declarations").

---

[1] In earlier releases of C++, nested classes are not local to their enclosing class's scope.

- Can be local to a function. The local class grants no special access permissions to nor can it use any automatic variables of the enclosing function.

  Member functions must be defined in the declaration (inline). (See "Member Functions.")

  Local classes may not have `static` data members (see "Data Members").

Example:
```
void Contrived() {
    int i;
    static s;

    class Local {
        // ...
    public:
        int f() { return i; }   // error: i is auto
        int g() { return s; }   // ok: s is static
    };
    // ...
}

Local vacuous;          // error: Local not in scope
```

Data Members...

- Are collections of related information, possibly of several types, combined into one object.

- Can be in the private, protected, or public parts of a class.

  Example[1]:
  ```
  home.area = 708;          // error: private
  home.handset = offHook;   // error: protected
  if ( home.OffHook() )     // ok
      home.GiveDialTone();
  ```

- Can be declared static (have static storage class). Static data members are shared by all objects of a class.

  They can be referred to by qualification to the class name (using the scope-resolution operator) and not to any specific object of that class.

  Static data members must be defined at file scope (somewhere). They may also be initialized; if not, they are initialized to zero (or equivalent)[2].

  Example:
  ```
  // Shape.h file
  class Shape {
      static int numShapes;       // declaration
      // ...
  };

  // Shape.c file
  int Shape::numShapes = 0;       // definition
  ```

---

[1] It is assumed that the example code is in a non-member or non-friend function. (See "Member Functions" or "Friend Functions," respectively.)

[2] Initial releases of C++ do not support definition nor initialization of static data members at file scope.

- Can be declared `const`. A `const` data member must be initialized in every constructor's definition[1] (see "Constructors"). The name of the data member, and its initial value enclosed in parentheses, is separated from the constructor's argument list by a colon.

  Example:
  ```
  class Phone {
      const int area, exchange, line;  // make const
      // ...
  public:
      Phone( int a, int e, int l )
      : area(a), exchange(e), line(l) {
          // ...
      }
      // ...
  };
  ```

- Can be variables of another class. These must be explicitly initialized if the data member's class has no default constructor (see "Constructors"). They are initialized in the same manner as `const` data members.

  Example:
  ```
  class Phone {
      // ...
  public:
      Phone( int, int, int ); // needs arguments
      // ...
  };

  class Car {            // Car class has a Phone in it
      // ...
      Phone phone;        // must be initialized
  public:
      Car( /* ... */ int a, int e, int l )
      : phone( a, e, l ) { /* ... */ }
      // ...
  };
  ```

---

[1] Classes with `const` data members must have at least one constructor to initialize them; the constructor's body can be an empty set of braces { }.

Member Functions...

- Are functions that manipulate data members.

- Have access to all members of their class automatically.

- Can be in the `private`, `protected`, or `public` parts of a class.

- Can be defined inside or outside of the `class` declaration on an individual basis[1]. When outside, they can still be made `inline`[2]. Also when outside, default arguments can not be respecified.

- Can refer to data members or member functions declared after them in the `class` declaration.

  Example:
  ```
  // IntStack.h file
  class IntStack {
      int *v, size, top;
  public:
      // ...
      int Top() const;              // deferred
      void Push( int );             // ditto
  };

  inline int IntStack::Top() const { return v[top]; }


  // IntStack.c file
  void IntStack::Push( int element ) {
      if ( top+1 < size ) v[ ++top ] = element;
  }
  ```

---

[1] Small, "one-liner" member functions are usually put in declarations; large member functions are put in .c files. Placement is left to the discretion of the user; however, implementations may impose restrictions on what kinds of statements may be in `inline` member functions. In such cases, the user is forced to put those definitions into a .c file.

[2] The member function declaration inside the `class` declaration may be preceded by the `inline` keyword to signify this; it has no use other than to serve as a readability aid.

- Have an implicitly declared variable `this` that is a constant pointer to the class object for which it was called. Most of the time, explicit use of `this` is unnecessary unless the pointer address itself is needed as is the case when doing linked lists.

Example:
```
class Node {
    // ...
    Node *next;
public:
    // ...
    void InsertAfter( Node* p ) {
        if ( this && p ) { // check for nil pointers
            next = p->next; // next is this->next
            p->next = this; // explicit use of this
        }
    }
};
```

Another use is to be able to chain multiple member function calls together. Returning a reference to the class object that the function was called for enables this to be done[1].

Example:
```
class Phone {
    // ...
public:
    Phone& GiveDialTone();  // return Phone& instead
    // ...
};

Phone& Phone::GiveDialTone() {
    // ...
    return *this;            // *this is a Phone&
}

Phone home( 516,555,8858 );

long digits = home.GiveDialTone().AcceptDigits();
// would previously had to have done...
// home.GiveDialTone();
// long digits = home.AcceptDigits();
```

---

[1] Other common uses for explicitly referencing `this` occur in constructors (see "Constructors") and in overloading the assignment operator (see "Assignment Operator" under "Operator Overloading").

- Can be declared `static` which only allows them to directly access and modify `static` data members[1]; `static` member functions can not be `const` nor `virtual`[2].

They can be referred to by qualification to the class name (using the scope-resolution operator) and not to any specific object of that class.

Example:
```
class Shape {
    static int numShapes;    // static data member
protected:
    Point center;
public:
    Shape( Point c ) : center( c ) { ++numShapes; }
    ~Shape() { --numShapes; }
    // ...
    static int NumShapes() { return numShapes; }
};
// ...
    for ( int n = Shape::NumShapes(); n > 0; --n )
        // ...
```

When defined outside the `class` declaration, the `static` keyword is not respecified.

Example:
```
class Shape {
    // ...
    static int NumShapes();        // defined later
};

// ...

inline int Shape::NumShapes() {  // no static here!
    return numShapes;
}
```

---

[1] Initial releases of C++ do not support `static` member functions.
[2] It follows that `static` member functions have no `this` pointer since `static` data members are not associated with any particular class object.

- Can be declared `const` which does not allow them to change the value of nor return a non-`const` reference or pointer to any data member[1]; `const` member functions can not be `static`.

Only `const` member functions can be called for `const` objects. (They can also be called for non-`const` objects.)

Example:
```
class IntStack {
    int *v, size, top;
public:
    // ...
    int Pop();
    int Top() const;   // does not modify anything
};

void f( const IntStack& s ) { // const object
    int a = s.Top();   // ok: Top() is const member
    int b = s.Pop();   // error: can't modify s
}
```

- Can be declared `volatile`. Only `volatile` member functions can be called for `volatile` objects. Member functions can be both `const` and `volatile`.

- Can be declared `virtual` (see "Virtual Member Functions" under "Derived Classes"); `virtual` member functions can not be `static`.

---

1 Initial releases of C++ do not support `const` member functions.

Pointers to Members...

- Point to a non-`static` data member or member function (`virtual` member functions included) for any object of a class[1]. (A pointer to a `static` data member is an ordinary pointer.)

  Example:
  ```
  struct Point { // see "Structure & Union Classes"
      int x, y;
      void Set( int x0, int y0 ) { x = x0, y = y0; }
  };

  Point a, *pa = &a;

  // pint is a pointer to any int member of Point
  int Point::*pint = &Point::x; // in this case, x

  // pmf2i is a pointer to any member function of
  // Point taking 2 int's and returning void
  void (Point::*pmf2i)( int, int ) = &Point::Set;

  ++(a.*pint);              // increment a's x
  ++(pa->*pint);            // increment a's x again
  (a.*pmf2i)( 1, 1 );       // call a's Set()
  (pa->*pmf2i)( 2, 2 );     // call a's Set() via pa
  ```

- Are implicitly converted to be pointers to members of a derived class when necessary. (See "Pointers" under "Derived Classes.")

- Are not implicitly converted to pointers to `void` like ordinary pointers are.

---

[1] A pointer to an `int` data member, say, is not a pointer to a specific `int`, but an offset into an object of a given class for the specified `int` data member. Initial releases of C++ do not support pointers to members.

Constructors...

- Initialize a class object from an optional argument list. Arguments, if used, may have default values.

- Are invoked automatically by the compiler when a variable of a class is declared, when a conversion is needed in expressions, function arguments or return-values, or when the `new` operator is called to create one in the free-store.

- Have all non-`virtual` base class constructors, if any, invoked before them (see "Base Class Constructors" and "Virtual Base Classes" under "Derived Classes").

- Have the same name as the class for which it is defined.

- Can be in the `private`, `protected`, or `public` parts of a class[1].

- Can be defined inside or outside of the `class` declaration on an individual basis (just like member functions).

    Example:
    ```
    class IntStack {
        int *v, size, top;
    public:
        IntStack( int ezis );          // declaration
        // ...
    };

    IntStack::IntStack( int ezis ) {   // definition
        v = new int[ size = ezis ];
        top = -1;
    }

    // declare IntStack; calls constructor
    IntStack huge( 1000 );
    ```

- Can not be declared `const`, `volatile`, `static`, nor `virtual`; can not have a return-type nor have their address taken.

---

[1] If a constructor is in the `private` part of a class, then only `friend` functions may create objects of that class using that constructor; if a constructor is in the `protected` part, then only `friend` functions or member functions of a derived class may create objects of that class using that constructor.

- Can be invoked in one of three ways, all being equal. (The choice is left to the preference of the user.)

  Example:
  ```
  IntStack good( 100 );
  IntStack bad = IntStack( 100 );   // explicit
  IntStack ugly = 100;              // shorthand
  ```

- Perform user-defined type conversions if they can take one argument (either because they have only one argument or because all the rest can have default values).

  Such conversions are used in addition to arithmetic conversions in expressions, initializations, and function arguments and return-values. (See "Arithmetic Conversions" under "Operators.")

  At most, one user-defined conversion, either by constructor or conversion operator, is performed. (See "Conversion Operators.")

  Example:
  ```
  class String { /* ... */ String( const char* ); };
  class BitString { /* ... */ BitString( String ); };

  void f( const String& s ) { /* ... */ }
  void g( const BitString& b ) { /* ... */ }
  // ...
      f( "Hello" );   // conversion: String( "Hello" )
      g( "10110" );   // error: conversion not tried
                      // BitString( String( "10110" ) )
  ```

- Are used to initialize `const` data members and data members that are variables of a class[1]. A `const` data member must be initialized in every constructor's definition[2]. The name of the data member, and its initial value enclosed in parentheses, is separated from the constructor's argument list by a colon. (Also see "Data Members.")

Example:
```
class IntStack {
    const int size;                   // const now
    // ...
};

IntStack::IntStack( int ezis ) : size( ezis ) {
    v = new int[ size ];
    top = -1;
}
```

- Are considered to be *default constructors* if they can take no arguments (either because they have no arguments or because they all can have default values)[3].

A default constructor is required when a vector of class objects is created using the `new` operator.

Example:
```
// want p to point to a vector of 5 IntStacks
IntStack *p = new IntStack[ 5 ];     // error

class IntStack {                     // modify IntStack class
    // ...
    IntStack( int = 20 );   // default constructor
    // ...
};

// each of 5 IntStacks has a size of 20
IntStack *p = new IntStack[ 5 ];     // ok now
```

---

1 Non-`const` data members may also be initialized this way. The choice is left to the preference of the user; however, when a data member is a variable of a class, this method of initialization is more efficient.

2 Classes with `const` data members must have at least one constructor; the constructor's body can be an empty set of braces { }.

3 If no constructors are declared for a class, the compiler automatically generates a default constructor that calls the constructors of any class data members, if any, and of base classes, if any.

- Are considered to be *copy constructors* if they can take one class reference argument of the class or a `const` class reference argument of the class (either because they have only one argument or because all the rest can have default values)[1].

  A copy constructor is used to construct a class object from another class object[2].

  A copy constructor should be defined if the class contains a data members that is a pointer to dynamically-allocated memory[3].

- Can be overloaded.

  Example:
  ```
  class IntStack {
      // ...
  public:
      IntStack( int = 10 );
      IntStack( const IntStack& );  // this is it
      // ...                        // also overloaded
  };

  IntStack::IntStack( const IntStack& from ) {
      v = new int[ size = from.size ];
      for ( register int i = 0; i < size; ++i )
          v[i] = from.v[i];
      top = from.top;
  }
      // ...
      IntStack a( 100 );
      IntStack b( a );  // declare b, make equal to a
      IntStack c = a;   // same thing, alternate form
  ```

---

1 That is, it has the signature X(X&) or X(const X&), the latter being preferred. If no copy constructor is declared for a class, the compiler automatically generates a default copy constructor that does a member-wise copy for all of its data members.

2 This constructor is also called when passing function arguments and return values by value.

3 If the copy constructor were not provided, then the default copy constructor would make b's v point to the same place as a's v in the example. For similar reasons, the assignment operator = should be overloaded whenever a copy constructor is user-defined (see "Assignment Operator" under "Operator Overloading"). Alternatively, initialization of a class object from another of the same class can be disallowed by merely *declaring* the copy constructor in the `private` part of the class.

- Can initialize vectors of class objects in the same way as vectors of built-in types[1]. A constructor is called for each vector element. If there is no constructor that can take one argument, then constructors must be explicitly specified.

The left-most number of elements can be omitted in which it equals the number of values. If the number of elements is given and the number of values is less than that, then the remaining elements are initialized using the default constructor[2]. If all the values for a size are given, then that set of braces can be omitted.

Examples:
```
// Vector of 4 stacks.  The first 3 have the sizes
// listed; the 4th has a size of 10 due to the
// default constructor.

IntStack polyStack[4] = { 5, 10, 15 /*, 10 */ };

// ...

Phone office[] = {           // no constructor that
    Phone( 708,555,8887 ),   // takes 1 argument, so
    Phone( 708,555,7245 )    // must use explicit
};

Phone office[3] = {          // error: needs default
    Phone( 708,555,6012 ),   // constructor that
    Phone( 708,555,3707 )    // Phone does not have
};
```

---

1 Earlier releases of C++ do not allow explicit element initialization.
2 If there is no default constructor, then all values must be specified.

Destructors...

- Perform any needed clean-up of an object before it's destroyed.

- Are invoked automatically by the compiler when a class variable goes out of scope, when a temporary object created for a conversion in an expression, function argument or return-value is no longer needed, or when the `delete` operator is called for one in the free-store.

- Have the same name as the class for which it is defined prefixed by the ~ (tilde) character, do not have a return-type, and can not take arguments; therefore, can not be overloaded.

- Can be `virtual` (see "Virtual Member Functions" under "Derived Classes").

Example:
```
class IntStack {
    int *v, size, top;
public:
    IntStack( int ezis = 20 );
    ~IntStack() { delete[] v; }    // destructor
    // ...
};
// ...
int main() {
    IntStack s( 100 );
    IntStack* ps = new IntStack( 50 );
    // ...
    delete ps;      // destructor called for ps
    // destructor called here implicitly for s
}
```

- Can be explicitly called using either of the member selection operators[1]. (The need to do this is rare.)

Example:
```
IntStack s( 100 ), *ps = new IntStack( 50 );
// ...
s.~IntStack();       // explicitly destroy s
this->~IntStack();   // explicitly destroy *this
```

---

[1] Earlier releases require that the destructor be explicitly qualified to the class's name using the class scope-resolution operator; initial releases of C++ do not support this at all.

Conversion Operators...

- Provide a mechanism to convert a `class` type into a built-in type or to a previously-defined `class` type.

- Have the form...

```
operator type() { /* ... */ }
```

...that is, have no explicit return-type nor arguments; therefore, can not be overloaded[1].

- Are used in addition to arithmetic conversions in expressions, initializations, and function arguments and return-values. (See "Arithmetic Conversions" under "Operators.")

Example:
```
class String {
    char *s;
public:
    // ...
    operator const char*() const { return s; }
};

void f( const char* s ) { /* ... */ }

String s;
// ...
    f( s );  // conversion: s.operator const char*()
```

At most, one user-defined conversion, either by conversion operator or constructor, is performed. (See "Constructors.")

Example:
```
class BitString { /* ... */ operator String(); };
BitString b;
// ...
    f( b );  // error: conversion not tried
    // b.operator String().operator const char*()
```

- Are inherited and can be `virtual` (see "Virtual Member Functions" under "Derived Classes").

---

1 There can be multiple conversion operators converting to different types.

Structure & Union Classes...

- Are just like `class` classes except that the keyword `struct` or `union` is used in the declaration.

- Have all members and base classes `public` by default as opposed to `private` by default for `class` classes[1].

    Example:
    ```
    // these two classes amount to the same thing

    class True : public X {        struct Imitator : X {
        int a;                         Imitator();
    protected:                         int g();
        int f();                   protected:
    public:                            int f();
        True();                    private:
        int g();                       int a;
    };                             };
    ```

- For `union` classes, behave just like regular unions, that is, any *one* of a collection of several types is stored any any one time.

    Union classes can not be used as or have base classes, therefore can not have `virtual` member functions; can not have `static` data members. An anonymous union class can not have `private` or `protected` data members, nor member functions.

---

[1]   The choice as to whether `class` classes or `struct` classes are used is left to the preference of the user. If all the members of a class are `public`, then the `struct` declaration might as well be used.

Friend Functions...

- Are functions that are granted access to the `private` parts of a class of which they are not a member and the `protected` parts of a class from which they are not derived.

- Can be friends of more than one class.

- Are declared within the `class` declaration for which the `friend` is being granted permission[1]. The argument types and return-type must be specified exactly as in the true `friend` function declaration.

Example:
```
class Person {
    int secret;                          // private
public:
    // ...
    friend void Spouse( Person& );    // non-member
};
// ...
void Spouse( Person& p ) {
    ++p.secret;         // can access private parts
}
```

- Can be declared for a member function of another class.

Example:
```
class Person {
    // ...
    friend void Family::Sibling();
    // Family::Sibling() is now a friend
};
```

- Can be declared for an entire class.

Example:
```
class Person {
    // ...
    friend class Family;
    // all member functions of Family are friends
};
```

---

1   It makes no difference whether `friend` declarations are in the `private`, `protected`, or `public` parts of a class.

- Are not transitive, that is, friends of friends of a class are not friends to that class.

  Example:
  ```
  class Family {
      friend class DistantRelative;
      // ...
  };

  class DistantRelative {
      void Pry( Person& p ) {
          ++p.secret;                      // error
          // DistantRelative is not a friend of Person
          // even though it is a friend of a friend
      }
  };
  ```

- Are not inherited by derived classes (see "Derived Classes").

  Example:
  ```
  class DistantRelative : public Family {
      void Pry( Person& p ) {
          ++p.secret;                      // error
          // DistantRelative is not a friend of Person
          // even though it is derived from a friend
      }
  };
  ```

Derived Classes...

- Provide a means to create a class that is a variation on a previously-defined class.

- Have access to the `public` and `protected` parts of its base classes.

Declaration...

- Introduces a new type.

- Establishes an access permission of `private`, `protected`, or `public` for the members of its base classes. Unless specified, `private` is assumed (although `public` is the most common).

  Private base classes have their `public` and `protected` members become `private` members of the derived class.

  Protected base classes have their `public` and `protected` members become `protected` members of the derived class[1].

  Public base classes have their `public` and `protected` members become `public` and `protected` members of the derived class, respectively.

  This can be represented graphically as shown below[2]:

	Base	**Derived**
Private	private $- - - - \to$ private	
	protected	protected
	public	public
Protected	private $- - - - \to$ private	
	protected $\longrightarrow$ protected	
	public	public
Public	private $- - - - \to$ private	
	protected $\longrightarrow$ protected	
	public $\longrightarrow$ public	

---

1   Protected base classes are only supported starting with the USL 3.0 release of C++.

2   The dashed line means that while the `private` data members of the base class become part of the derived class, they can not be accessed by it.

- Is just like that for regular classes, but also lists its base classes, along with their access permissions, following a colon.

Example:

```
class Phone {  // refer to the declaration of the
    // ...       // Phone class under "Classes"
};

// PayPhone has a Phone as a public base class
class PayPhone : public Phone {
    int centsDeposited;
public:
    PayPhone( int area, int exchange, int line );
    void  GiveDialTone();
    int   AcceptCoins();
};

// declare derived class variable
PayPhone booth( 708,555,5444 );
```

Member Functions...

- In a derived class, can override a base class's member function of the same name.

  The number and types of arguments and the return-type of the derived class's member function may differ from that of the base class's.

  Example:
  ```
  class PayPhone : public Phone {
      // ...
  public:
      // ...
      void GiveDialTone(); // as declared previously
  };

  Phone home( 516,555,8858 );
  PayPhone booth( 708,555,5444 );

  // ...

  home.GiveDialTone();     // Phone::GiveDialTone()
  booth.GiveDialTone();    // PayPhone::GiveDialTone()
  ```

- Can call the base class's member function using the scope-resolution operator.

  Example:
  ```
  void PayPhone::GiveDialTone() {
      // do something extra for a PayPhone...
      Phone::GiveDialTone();   // call original[1]
  }
  ```

---

[1] If this were not done, a recursive call would result.

Access Declarations...

- Enable the `protected` and `public` members of a `private` base class to be made `protected` or `public` again, respectively, in the derived class.

- Enable the `public` members of a `protected` base class to be made `public` again in the derived class[1].

- For overloaded member functions of a given name, enable all of them to be restored to their former access permission provided they all have the same access permission in the base class.

Example:
```
class Base {
    int a;
    void g();    // note different access for g()'s
public:
    int b, c;
    void f(), f(int), g(int);
};

class Derived : private Base {
    // ...
public:
    Base::a;    // error: can't make 'a' public
    Base::b;    // restore Base's b to public
    int c;
    Base::c;    // error: two declarations of c
    Base::f;    // restore all of Base's f()'s
    Base::g;    // error: g()'s not the same
};
```

Pointers & References...

- For a base class, point or refer to an object of a derived class.

(See the example under "Virtual Member Functions.")

----

[1] Neither this nor the previous item can be done if the derived class declares a member with the same name as a member in the base class.

Virtual Member Functions...

- Enable member functions with the same name to be selected based on the *type of the class object pointed to* and *not* the type of the pointer.

- Enable the *object-oriented* programming paradigm to be used.

- Can not differ in the number and types of arguments nor the return-type from that of the base class's member function; if they do, the `virtual` mechanism is suppressed.

- Can not be `static`.

Example:
```
class Phone {
    // ...
public:
    // ...
    virtual void GiveDialTone();   // make virtual
    // ...
};

class PayPhone : public Phone {   // no changes
    int centsDeposited;
public:
    PayPhone( int area, int exchange, int line );
    void  GiveDialTone();
    int   AcceptCoins();
};

// ...

Phone home( 516,555,8858 );
PayPhone booth( 708,555,5444 );
Phone *p;               // pointer to any kind of Phone

p = &home;              // no surprises here...
p->GiveDialTone(); // call Phone::GiveDialTone()

p = &booth;             // and now for some magic...
p->GiveDialTone(); // call PayPhone::GiveDialTone()
```

- Can be used to make *abstract base classes*[1]. An abstract base class is a class that contains at least one *pure virtual member function.* A pure virtual member function is a `virtual` member function that declares the function's interface but leaves the implementation to a derived class[2]. This is done by setting the member function declaration equal to zero.

Example:
```
struct Point {
    int x, y;
    Point( int x0=0, int y0=0 ) { x = x0, y = y0; }
};

class Shape {          // abstract base class
protected:
    Point center;
public:
    Shape( Point c ) : center( c ) {}
    virtual Shape& Draw() const = 0; // pure virtual
};

class Circle : public Shape {
    int radius;
public:
    Circle( Point c, int r = 1 );
    Shape& Draw() const;       // will define Draw()
};
// ...
Shape amorphous;       // error: abstract class
Circle c;
Shape *p = &c;         // ok: pointer to any Shape
```

A *pure* `virtual` member function should never be called directly or indirectly from a constructor.

---

1   The destructor of an abstract base class should always be `virtual`. Initial releases of C++ do not support abstract base classes.
2   No objects of an abstract base class can be declared; only objects of derived classes for which all pure virtual member functions have been defined can be declared.

- Can be called from a constructor directly or indirectly via a non-virtual member function; however, the function called will be its own class's version, or that of its base class's, if any, and never any derived class's version.

Example:
```
class Phone {
    // ...
public:
    Phone( int a, int e, int l ) {
        // ...
        AcceptDigits();          // this always calls
    }
    virtual void GiveDialTone();  // this function
    long AcceptDigits() {
        // ...                    // despite the indirect
        GiveDialTone();           // call though here...
    }
    // ...
};

class PayPhone : public Phone {
    // ...
public:
    // ...
    void GiveDialTone();      // ...and never this one
};
```

Base Class Constructors...

- Are invoked before derived class constructors.

- Must be explicitly invoked in every derived class constructor's definition if the base class does not have a default constructor[1].

  The name of the base class constructor[2], and its arguments enclosed in parentheses, is separated from the derived class constructor's name by a colon[3]. Multiple base class constructors are separated by commas (see "Multiple Base Classes").

  Example:
  ```
  class Phone {
      // ...
  public:
      Phone( int, int, int );    // needs arguments
      // ...
  };

  class PayPhone : public Phone {
      // ...
  public:
      PayPhone(int a, int e, int l) : Phone(a, e, l) {
          // ...
      }
      // ...
  };
  ```

- Can call non-pure `virtual` member functions directly or indirectly via a non-`virtual` member function; however, the function called will be its own version, or that of its base class's, if any, and never any derived class's version. (See "Virtual Member Functions.")

- Should *never* call pure `virtual` member functions directly or indirectly (see "Virtual Member Functions").

---

1 This means that even if a derived class needs no constructor for itself, it still must provide one to invoke its base classes' constructors that require arguments; the body of the derived class's constructor would be an empty set of braces { }.

2 Initial releases of C++ do not allow the name to be specified.

3 Just like const data members (see "Data Members" under "Classes").

Base Class Destructors...

• Are invoked after derived class destructors.

• Can be `virtual`. The destructor of an abstract base class should always be `virtual`.

• Can call `virtual` member functions directly or indirectly via a non-`virtual` member function; however, the function called will be its own version, or that of its base class's, if any, and never any derived class's version.

Multiple Base Classes...

• Allow a class to be derived from more than one class[1]. The order in which base classes are listed generally doesn't matter[2].

• Must have base class members with the same name qualified with the name of one of the base classes using the scope-resolution operator.

Example:
```
class A { public: void f(); /* ... */ };
class B { public: void f(); /* ... */ };
class C : public A, public B { /* ... */ };
// ...
    C c;
    c.f();          // error: which f()?  A's or B's?
    c.A::f();       // ok: qualified
```

It's often best to resolve such ambiguities in the derived class by overriding both functions.

Example:
```
class C : public A, public B {
    // ...
public:
    void f() { A::f(); B::f(); }  // override both
    // ...
};
// ...
    C c;
    c.f();              // ok now
```

---

[1] Initial releases of C++ do not support multiple base classes.
[2] It matters if the user has the base classes' constructors or destructors modifying global data.

- For a class derived from derived classes with a common base, there exists two instances of the common base, by default.

    Example:
    ```
    struct X { int i; /* ... */ X(int); };

    class A : public X { /* ... */ A(int); };
    class B : public X { /* ... */ B(int); };
    class C : public A, public B { /* ... */ C(int); };
    ```

    This can be represented graphically as shown below:

    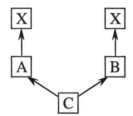

    Members in the common base class must be qualified with the name of one of the derived classes using the scope-resolution operator.

    Examples:
    ```
    C c(0);
    ++c.i;            // error: which i?  A's or B's?
    ++c.A::i;         // ok: qualified

    C* cp = new C(0);
    X* xp = cp;       // error: which X?
    X* xp = (A*)cp;   // ok: qualified
    ```

Virtual Base Classes...

- For a class derived from derived classes with a *virtual* common base, there exists only one instance of the common base.

- Are declared by including the `virtual` keyword with the base class's access permission specifier[1].

Example:
```
struct V { int i; /* ... */ V(int); };

class A : virtual public V { /* ... */ A(int); };
class B : virtual public V { /* ... */ B(int); };
class C : public A, public B { /* ... */ C(int); };
```

This can be represented graphically as shown below:

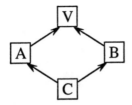

To access members in the common base class, no qualification is needed since there is only one instance.

In the case where a `virtual` base class and a derived class share a name of either a data member, member function, or an enumeration, the one in the derived class *dominates* the one in the `virtual` base class.

Example:
```
struct V { int i; void f(); /* ... */ };
struct A : virtual V { int i; int f(); /* ... */ };
struct B : virtual V { /* ... */ };

class C : public A, public B {
    // ...
    void g() { i = f(); }    // ok
    // both A::i and A::f() dominate V::i and V::f()
};
```

---

1 It doesn't matter whether the `virtual` keyword comes before or after the access specification.

- Have their constructors, if any, invoked by a constructor of the *most-derived* class.

  Example:
  ```
  V::V( int n ) : i(n) { /* ... */ }
  A::A( int i ) : V(i) { /* ... */ }
  B::B( int i ) : V(i) { /* ... */ }
  C::C( int i ) : V(i), A(i), B(i) { /* ... */ }
  ```

- Can be mixed with non-`virtual` base classes in a class's declaration.

- Can introduce unwanted multiple calls of a member function in a `virtual` base class.

  Example:
  ```
  class V {
      // ...
  public:
      void f() { /* ... */ }
      // ...
  };

  class A : virtual public V {
      // ...
  public:
      void f() { /* ... */ V::f(); }
      // ...
  };

  class B : virtual public V {
      // ...
  public:
      void f() { /* ... */ V::f(); }
      // ...
  };

  class C : public A, public B {
      // ...
  public:
      void f() { /* ... */ A::f(); B::f(); }
      // note: V::f() is called twice!
  };
  ```

One technique to account for this is to make `f()` a front-end for another function, say `real_f()`, that does the real work of `f()` for its class; `f()` will call the appropriate `real_f()`'s.

Example:
```
class V {
   // ...
protected:
   void real_f() { /* ... */ }
   // ...
public:
   void f() { real_f(); }
};

class A : virtual public V {
   // ...
protected:
   void real_f() { /* ... */ }
   // ...
public:
   void f() { real_f(); V::f(); }
   // ...
};

class B : virtual public V {
   // ...
protected:
   void real_f() { /* ... */ }
   // ...
public:
   void f() { real_f(); V::f(); }
   // ...
};

class C : public A, public B {
   // ...
protected:
   void real_f() { /* ... */ }
   // ...
public:
   void f() {
      real_f();
      A::real_f(); B::real_f(); V::real_f();
   }
   // ...
};
```

Templates...

- Extend the function and class concepts by providing a means to *parameterize* them, that is, declare functions and classes in terms of "any type."[1]

Function Templates...

- Are function declarations prefixed by a *template specification.* A template specification consists of the keyword `template` followed by a parameter list enclosed in angle brackets `< >`.

- Have type parameters designated by the `class` keyword followed by an identifier[2]; the identifier serves as a place-holder for the type name. There can be more than one type parameter.

- Are *automatically* expanded into full function definitions as needed by the compiler.

  Example:
  ```
  // declaration: Max of two T's
  template<class T> const T& Max(const T&, const T&);
  // ...
      template<class T> const T&     // definition³
  Max( const T& a, const T& b ) {
     return a > b ? a : b;
  }
  // ...
     int i, j;
     float a, b;
     // ...
     int k = Max( i, j );     // call Max(int,int)
     float c = Max( a, b );   // call Max(float,float)
  ```

- Can be overloaded with other `template` or non-`template` functions.

  Example:
  ```
  template<class T> const T& Max(const T&, const T&);
  template<class T> const T& Max(const T*, int);
  int Max( int (*)( int ), int (*)( int ) );
  ```

---

1 Templates are only supported starting with the USL 3.0 release of C++.
2 The `class` keyword in the context of templates has a broader meaning of *any* type, not just that of a class.
3 In order for this example to work for a type T where T is a class type, the > operator must be overloaded in that class; if not, a link-time error will occur.

- Can be provided for specific types to override the use of the
  `template` to do (not do) something that the `template` function
  does not (does).

Example:
```
    const char*&
Max( const char*& c, const char*& d ) {
    // ...do something special with char*'s...
}
```

Class Templates...

- Are `class` declarations prefixed by a `template` specification.

- Are *automatically* expanded into full `class` declarations as needed by the compiler.

- Can not be nested within other classes (unlike ordinary classes).

   Example:
   ```
   // declare a Stack for any type T
   template<class T> class Stack {
       T *v;                // pointer to some type T
       int size, top;
   public:
       Stack( int ezis );
       ~Stack();
       void Push( const T& );    // push a T
       T& Pop();                 // pop a T
       T& Top() const;           // etc.
   };

   Stack<int> i;       // declare i as a stack of int
   Stack<char*> cp;    // declare cp as a stack of char*
   ```

- Can have non-type (or only non-type) parameters. The values specified for such parameters must be constant expressions.

   Example:
   ```
   // pass size as a template parameter¹
   template<class T, int size> class Stack {
       T v[ size ];             // vector of some type T
       int top;
   public:
       Stack() : top( -1 ) {}
       // ...
   };

   Stack<int,20> tiny;       // pass along sizes
   Stack<int,500> huge;
   ```

The stacks `tiny` and `huge`, although both are stacks of `int`, are of two completely different types because of the different sizes. To

---

1   The advantage of using a non-type parameter in this case is that the data member v is allocated without the use of the new operator and the potential for it to fail.

illustrate, a pointer to a `Stack<int,20>` is *not* also a pointer to a `Stack<int,500>`.

Example:
```
Stack<int,20>* is20p = &tiny;       // ok
Stack<int,500>* is500p = &tiny;     // error
```

- Can be derived from both non-`template` and `template` classes; can have both non-`template` and `template` classes derived from them[1].

Example:
```
class A { /* ... */ };
template<class T> class B : public A {/* ... */};
template<class T> class C : public B<T> {/*...*/};
class D : public C<int> { /* ... */ };
```

- Can be provided for specific types of a class to override the use of the `template` to do (not do) something that the `template` class does not (does). The entire class must be respecified in terms of specific types and values.

Example:
```
// declare our own Stack for char*
class Stack<char*> {
    char* *v;                // pointer to char*
    int size, top;
public:
    Stack( int ezis );
    ~Stack();
    void Push( const char*& );
    char*& Pop();
    char*& Top() const;
};
```

- Can also be of structure and union classes (see "Structure & Union Classes" under "Classes").

---

[1] When a non-`template` class is derived from a `template` class, all the `template` class's parameters must be given "real" types and values, `int` in the example.

Static Data Members...

- Are shared by all objects of a class for *each instantiation* of the `template` class.

- Are defined at file scope (as all `static` data members must be) by prefixing the definition by a `template` specification.

  Example:
  ```
  template<class T> class C {
      static int i;   // ordinary static data member
      static T t;     // parameterized
      // ...
  };

  template<class T> int C<T>::i;   // define at
  template<class T> T C<T>::t;     // file scope
  // ...
  C<char> c;          // has int C::i and char C::t
  C<float> f;         // has int C::i and float C::t
  ```

Member Function Templates...

- Are defined outside their `class` declaration by prefixing them with a `template` specification.

  Example:
  ```
      template<class T> void
  Stack<T>::Push( const T& element ) {
      if ( top == size - 1 )
          error( "stack overflow" );
      else
          v[ ++top ] = element;
  }
  ```

- Can be provided for specific types of a class to override the use of the `template` to do (not do) something that the `template` member function does not (does).

  Example:
  ```
      void
  Stack<char*>::Push( const char*& ccpr ) {
      // ...do something special with char*'s...
  }
  ```

Friend Functions...

- For every type T, can be friends of all classes of type T; such friend functions are ordinary friend functions.

- For a type T, can be friends of a class of that T.

- Can be prefixed by a template specification. For types T and U, template functions of type U are friends of every class of type T.

Example:
```
template<class T> class Person {
    friend void Pet();
    friend void Spouse( Person<T>& );
    template<class U> friend void Coworker( U& );
};
// ...
void Pet() { /* ... */ }    // ordinary function

    template<class T> void
Spouse( Person<T>& p ) { /* ... */ }

    template<class U> void
Coworker( U& u ) { /* ... */ }
```

Here, for every type T, Pet() is a friend of Person<T>.

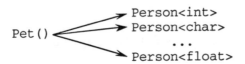

```
                        ⟋ Person<int>
Pet() ⟨=====⟩ Person<char>
                           ...
                        ⟍ Person<float>
```

For any type T, say, int, Spouse(Person<int>&) is a friend of Person<int>, but not Person<char> or any other type.

```
Spouse( Person<int>& )   ⟶ Person<int>
Spouse( Person<char>& )  ⟶ Person<char>
        ...                      ...
Spouse( Person<float>& ) ⟶ Person<float>
```

For every type T and every type U, Coworker(U&) is a friend of Person<T>.

```
Coworker( int& )   ⟍   ⟋ Person<int>
Coworker( char& )  ⟩⟨  Person<char>
        ...        ⟋ ⟍      ...
Coworker( float& ) ⟋   ⟍ Person<float>
```

- Can be declared for a member function of another class.

  Example:
  ```
  template<class T> class Person {
      // ...
      friend void Family::Sibling();
      friend void Acquaintance<T>::Casual(Person<T>&);
      template<class U> friend void
          Neighbor<U>::NextDoor( U& );
  };
  ```

  Here, for every type T, `Family::Sibling()` is a friend of `Person<T>`.

  For any type T, say, `int`,
  `Acquaintance<int>::Casual( Person<int>& )` is a friend of `Person<int>`, but not `Person<char>` or any other type.

  For every type T every any type U,
  `Neighbor<U>::NextDoor( U& )` is a friend of `Person<T>`.

- Can be declared for an entire class.

  Example:
  ```
  template<class T> class Person {
      // ...
      friend class Family;
      friend class Acquaintance<T>;
      template<class U> friend class Neighbor;
  };
  ```

  Here, for every type T, all member functions of `Family` are friends of `Person<T>`.

  For any type T, say, `int`, all member functions of `Acquaintance<int>` are friends of `Person<int>`, but not `Person<char>` or any other type.

  For every type T and every type U, all member functions of `Neighbor<U>` are friends of `Person<T>`.

- Can also be friends of non-`template` classes.

Operator Overloading...

- Allows any operator except ::, sizeof, ?:, ., and .* to have its meaning extended for class types[1].

- Is done by declaring a function with a name consisting of the keyword operator followed by one of the built-in operators[2].

- Makes no assumptions about similar operators. For example, if i is an int, ++i means i+=1, which means i=i+1. For overloaded operators, there are no such equivalences unless the user defines them.

- Can not use default arguments.

Unary Operators...

- Can be declared as non-static member functions taking no arguments. That is, for any operator @, @x is interpreted as x.operator@().

- Can be declared as non-member functions taking one argument that must be a class variable or a reference to one. That is, for any operator @, @x is interpreted as operator@(x)[3].

Examples:
```
class X {
    X operator-() const;      // unary minus
    X operator&() const;      // unary & (address of)
    X operator^() const;      // error: unary ^
};

class Y {
    friend Y operator-(const Y&);    // unary minus
    friend Y operator&(const Y&);    // unary &
    friend Y operator^(const Y&);    // error
};
```

---

1 It does not allow the precedence, associativity, nor the number of operands for an operator to be changed; nor does not allow operator semantics for built-in types to be changed.

2 You can't create new operators.

3 The choice as to whether most unary operators are members is left to the user although they are generally declared as such.

Binary Operators...

- Can be declared as non-`static` member functions taking one argument. That is, for any operator @, x@y is interpreted as x.operator@(y).

- Can be declared as non-member functions taking two arguments; one must be a class variable or a reference to one[1]. That is, for any operator @ except =, x@y is interpreted as operator@(x,y).

Examples:
```
class X {
    X operator-(const X&) const;   // binary minus
    X operator&(const X&) const;   // binary & (and)
    X operator!(const X&) const;   // error: binary !
};

class Y {
    friend Y operator-(const Y&, const Y&);
    friend Y operator&(const Y&, const Y&);
    friend Y operator!(const Y&, const Y&); // error
};
```

Function Call Operator...

- Must be defined as a non-`static` member function.

- Allows the user to define the number of operands.

Example:
```
class X {
    // ...
public:
    X( int a, int b, int c );
    // ...
    void operator()( int i, int j, int k );
};

X Xample( 1, 2, 3 );     // constructor called
Xample( 4, 5, 6 );       // operator() called
```

---

[1] Binary operators are generally declared as nonmembers (most often friends). Doing so allows expressions containing class variables and overloaded operators to be commutative.

Assignment Operator...

- Is used to assign the value of one class object to another.

- Unless defined by the user, has an implicit definition that does a member-wise assignment for all data members.

- Should be user-defined when a class contains a data member that is a pointer to dynamically-allocated memory[1].

- Is the only operator function that is *not* inherited.

- Must be defined as a non-`static` member function.

Example:
```
class IntStack {
    int *v, size, top;
public:
    // ...
    IntStack& operator=( const IntStack& );
};

    IntStack&
IntStack::operator=( const IntStack& from ) {
    if ( this != &from ) {   // check for from = from
        delete[] v;
        v = new int[ size = from.size ];
        for ( register int i = 0; i < size; ++i )
            v[i] = from.v[i];
        top = from.top;
    }
    return *this;       // allows multiple assignments
}

    // ...
    IntStack a( 100 ), b, c;
    // ...
    c = b = a;          // assign a to b and c
```

---

1 If the assignment operator were not overloaded, then the default assignment operator would make b's v point to the same place as a's v in the example. For similar reasons, a copy constructor should be defined whenever the assignment operator is overloaded (see "Constructors" under "Classes"). Alternatively, assignment to a class object from another of the same class can be disallowed by merely *declaring* the assignment operator in the `private` part of the class.

Subscript Operator...

• Must be defined as a non-`static` member function.

• Is most often declared to return a reference thus allowing it to appear on both sides of an assignment.

   Example[1]:
```
class String {
    char *s;
    // ...
public:
    String( char );
    String( const char* );
    char& operator[]( int pos ) { return s[ pos ]; }
    // ...
};

String ball = "mitten";
ball[0] = 'k';          // char& allows assignment
```

Member Access Operator[2]...

• For x->m, is interpreted as (x.operator->())->m[3]. Note that it is a *unary* operator and that x is a class object and *not* a pointer to one.

• Must return a pointer to a class object, or an object of or a reference to a class for which `operator->()` is defined since the original meaning of -> is not lost, just deferred.

• Must be defined as a non-`static` member function.

---

[1] In a real definition of `String`, the pos passed to `operator[]` would be checked for validity.

[2] Initial releases of C++ do not allow this to be overloaded.

[3] This does not apply to the binary operator ->*; nothing is special about it.

Increment & Decrement Operators...

- Can be overloaded for both prefix and postfix semantics[1].

<u>Prefix</u>: Is declared by a member operator having no arguments or a friend operator having one class or class-reference argument.

<u>Postfix</u>: Is declared by a member operator having one `int` argument or a friend operator having one class or class-reference argument and one `int` argument[2].

Example:
```
class X {
    // ...
public:
    X& operator++();        // prefix
    X& operator++(int);     // postfix
};

class Y {
    // ...
public:
    friend Y& operator--( Y& );        // prefix
    friend Y& operator--( Y&, int );   // postfix
};
```

1 Earlier releases of C++ provided no mechanism to distinguish between prefix and postfix.
2 The `int` argument is not really used; the value actually passed is zero.

New & Delete Operators...

• Provide a mechanism for a class to manage its own memory[1].

• Must have return-type `void*` for `new` and `void` for `delete`.

• Require a parameter of type `size_t` defined in the standard header file `<stddef.h>`.

• Are implicitly `static` member functions; therefore, can not be `const` nor `virtual`.

Example:
```
#include <stddef.h>        /* need this for size_t */

class Thing {
    // ...
    enum { block = 20 };
    static Thing *freeList;
public:
    // ...
    void* operator new( size_t );
    void  operator delete( void*, size_t );
};

void* Thing::operator new( size_t size ) {
    Thing *p;
    if ( !freeList ) {
        freeList = p = (Thing*)new char[size*block];
        while ( p != &freeList[ block-1 ] )
                p->next = p+1, ++p;
        p->next = 0;
    }
    p = freeList, freeList = freeList->next;
    return p;
}

void Thing::operator delete( void* p, size_t ) {
    ((Thing*)p)->next = freeList;
    freeList = (Thing*)p;
}
```

• When defined for a class, are *not* called when vectors of class objects are allocated or deallocated.

---

[1] Initial releases of C++ do not allow the `new` and `delete` operators to be overloaded.

- For the `new` operator, can be overloaded to accept more
  arguments. The arguments are passed by supplying them
  immediately after the `new` keyword enclosed in parentheses.

Example:
```
class Thing {
    // ...
public:
    // ...
    /*
    ** supply an additional argument buf to be used
    ** to allocate memory for a Thing at a specific
    ** memory address
    */
    void* operator new( size_t size, void* buf );
};
// ...
void* Thing::new( size_t size, void* buf ) {
    // allocate Thing at address pointed to be buf
}
    // ...
    char buffer[ 10000 ];
    Thing* p = new( buffer ) Thing;
```

Overloading the `new` operator with more arguments hides the
global `::operator new`; this will cause an error if the ordinary
`new` syntax is attempted.

Example:
```
Thing* p = new Thing;    // error: missing argument
```

To regain the use of the ordinary `new` syntax, a version of `new`
that accepts a single `size_t` argument must be provided; it just
has to call the global `::operator new`.

Example:
```
class Thing {
    // ...
    void* operator new( size_t size, void* buf );
    void* operator new( size_t size ) {
        return ::operator new( size );
    }
};
```

Preprocessor

This section describes the C++ preprocessor. Although is not part of the C++ language proper, virtually all C++ programs make use of it.

The C++ preprocessor is based on the ANSI C preprocessor. In many C++ implementations, however, an ANSI C, or even a "Classic C" preprocessor is used. One place that this fact can cause trouble is with comments.

Lines on which a # is the first non-white character are preprocessor directive lines. Directive lines are terminated by the newline character. Backslashes (\) just before newlines can be used to continue directive lines onto succeeding lines.

Comments...

- As mentioned previously, can cause trouble with older preprocessors since they do not recognize the C++ // comment.

Example:
```
#define  SIZE  256        // size of something
// ...
   for (int i=0; i < SIZE; ++i)
      // ...

// after non-C++ preprocessing...

   for (int i=0; i < 256 // size of something; ++i)
      // most likely a syntax error at this point
```

The // comment, instead of getting removed, is substituted right along with the rest of the line.

To avoid this regardless of whether a C++ preprocessor is being used, it's best to use only /* ... */ comments on preprocessor directive lines.

Example:
```
#define  SIZE  256        /* size of something */

   for (int i=0; i < 256; ++i)
      // as intended
```

Predefined Names...

• Contain various information during compilation.

`__cplusplus`	Defined by all C++ implementations.
`__LINE__`	Current line number of source-file.
`__FILE__`	Current source-file name.
`__DATE__`	Current date: `Mmm dd yyyy`
`__TIME__`	Current time: `hh:mm:ss`

Null Directive...

• Consists of a single #.

• Has no effect.

`#line` *constant* "*filename*"

• Permits the line number and filename that the compiler thinks it's compiling to be changed[1].

The constant becomes the current line number (`__LINE__`) and the filename becomes the current filename (`__FILE__`); the filename is optional.

`#include` <*filename*>
`#include` "*filename*"

• Includes the entire text of a file into the current file[2].

The first form looks for the file in a set of standard directories defined by an implementation of C++ on a given system; the second form looks in the current directory first.

Examples:
```
#include <iostream.h>   /* standard places */
#include "MyHeader.h"   /* this directory first */
```

`#pragma` *text*

• Instructs the implementation to take a particular implementation-dependent action. Unrecognized text is ignored.

---

1 This is mostly done by systems programs (such as the C++ compiler).
2 Files can include other files up to some implementation-dependent number.

#define *identifier text*
#define *identifier(identifier, ...) text*

- In its first form, associates *identifier* with *text* so that whenever *identifier* is encountered later on in the program it will be replaced with *text*[1].

  Example:
  ```
  #define forever for(;;)
  // ...
     forever {              // loop forever
        // ...
     }
  ```

- In its second form, it allows arguments[2]. There can not be space between the first *identifier* and the (.

  Identifiers in *text* should be enclosed in parentheses to ensure proper substitution.

  Example: `#define MIN(a,b)  ( (a)<(b) ? (a):(b) )`

  However, within *text*, identifiers will not be substituted if they are within quotes. This ensures that parts of literal text are not substituted. To override this, the # operator can be used.

  Example:
  ```
  #define MAIL(logid) "/usr/mail/" #logid
  // ...
  ifstream mailFile( MAIL( pjl ) );
  // MAIL( pjl ) becomes "/usr/mail/" "pjl" which
  // then gets concatenated to "/usr/mail/pjl"
  ```

#undef *identifier*

- Disassociates *identifier* from any previously associated text.

  Example: `#undef MIN`

#error *text*

- Causes the implementation to generate a message containing *text*.

---

[1]   The addition of `const` declarations has mostly outmoded this use of `#define` as used in C.

[2]   The addition of `inline` functions has mostly outmoded this use of `#define` as used in C.

Conditional Compilation...

- Permits sections of source code to be compiled (or not compiled) based upon external conditions.

- Begins in one of three ways:

```
#if   constant-expression    /* true? */
#ifdef identifier            /* defined? */
#ifndef identifier           /* not defined? */
```

For `#if`, *constant-expression* is evaluated and, if true (non-zero), all the source code up to a `#else`, `#elif`, or a `#endif` is compiled.

For `#ifdef` (and `#ifndef`), the subsequent source code is compiled if *identifier* has been previously defined (not defined).

The `defined` operator can be used within *constant-expression* to test if *identifier* has been previously defined; `!defined` can also be used to test if *identifier* has not been previously defined[1].

- Can have "else" sections in one of two forms:

```
#else
#elif constant-expression
```

For `#else`, the subsequent source code is compiled if the preceding `#if` (all-forms) evaluated to false.

For `#elif`, it's the same as for `#else` but *constant-expression* must also evaluate to true.

- Ends with: `#endif`

---

[1]　Earlier preprocessors lacked the `defined` operator, hence the existence of `#ifdef` and `#ifndef`. These are still supported for compatibility. (Also `#ifdef` requires less typing then `#if defined`.)

Examples:
```
#ifdef DEBUG
cerr << "counter = " << counter << endl;
#endif

#if defined SYSV
extern long f();
#elif defined BSD
extern short f();
#else
extern int f();
#endif
```

- Is often used to prevent header (".h") files from being included multiple times.

Example:
```
// Phone.h                  // PayPhone.h

#ifndef _PHONE_             #ifndef _PAYPHONE_
#define _PHONE_             #define _PAYPHONE_

class Phone {               #include "Phone.h"
   // ...
};                          class PayPhone : public Phone {
                               // ...
#endif                      };

                            #endif
```

```
// my.c
#include "Phone.h"
#include "PayPhone.h"
// ...
```

(See the following page for an explanation.)

Here, `my.c` needs the `Phone` class in the `Phone.h` header file and the `PayPhone` class in the `PayPhone.h` file.

The first `#include` in `my.c` includes `Phone.h`; in `Phone.h`, the identifier `_PHONE_` has not been defined so it gets defined and continues, declaring the `Phone` class.

The second `#include` in `my.c` includes `PayPhone.h`; in `PayPhone.h`, the identifier `_PAYPHONE_` has not been defined so it gets defined and continues. The `PayPhone` class needs the `Phone` class as well since a `PayPhone` is derived from a `Phone`; so it `#includes` the `Phone.h` file for itself. In `Phone.h` for the second time, the identifier `_PHONE_` has been defined so the remainder of the file is skipped.

If this mechanism were not used, the compiler would complain that the `Phone` class was multiply defined the second time around.

I/O Library

There are no input nor output facilities in C++; rather, I/O is handled via stream class libraries[1]. To use these facilities, you must #include the appropriate header files in your program[2].

Classes

- There are several classes in the I/O library; they are:

ios	base stream class
istream	input stream class
ostream	output stream class
iostream	input and output stream class
ifstream	input file stream class
ofstream	output file stream class
fstream	input and output file stream class

- Their relationships, in terms of derived classes, is represented below:

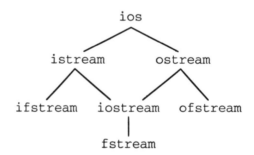

---

[1] The stdio library used with C is also supported, but has been mostly outmoded by the new C++ libraries.

[2] Not all header files are supported on all implementations.

Error States...

- Are internally maintained for every stream.

- Are stored as a collection of bits: `eofbit`, `failbit`, and `badbit`; multiple states are composed using the bitwise-or operator.

`int eof()`

- Returns true if the stream has encountered the end-of-file.

`int bad()`

- Returns true if some operation on a stream has failed; recovery from this condition is unlikely.

`int fail()`

- Returns true if some operation, such as an extraction or conversion, on a stream has failed; recovery from this is possible and the stream is still useable once the fail condition is cleared. Also returns true if `bad()` is true (but then recovery is not likely).

`int good()`

- Returns true if `eof()`, `bad()`, and `fail()` are all false.

`int rdstate()`

- Returns the current error state.

`void clear( int state )`

- Sets the error state of a stream.

   Example:
   ```
   istream s;
   // turn on failbit leaving others intact
   s.clear( ios::failbit | s.rdstate() );
   ```

`int operator!()`

`operator void*()`

- The former returns true if the `failbit` or the `badbit` is set; the latter returns false if the `failbit` or the `badbit` is set.

   Examples:
   ```
   if ( !myStream )  // operator!()
   if ( myStream )   // operator void*()
   ```

Stream Output...

- Is achieved by using a variable of the `ostream` or `iostream` class.

- Can be applied to one of the predefined output streams or to a user-defined output stream. The predefined output streams are:

cout	an `ostream` tied to standard output
cerr	an `ostream` tied to standard error

Insertion Operator...

- Writes a sequence of characters onto a specified stream.

- Is the `<<` operator overloaded[1].

- Is predefined for all simple types and pointers to `char` and `void`.

    Examples:
    ```
    cout << "Wow!  This is neat!\n";
    cerr << "Bad operand: " << op << '\n';
    ```

- Can be overloaded for `class` types[2].

    Example:
    ```
    class Phone {
        int area, exchange, line;
        // ...
        friend ostream& operator<<(
            ostream&, const Phone&
        );
    };

    ostream& operator<<(ostream& os, const Phone& p) {
        os << '(' << p.area << ") "
        << p.exchange << '-' << p.line;
        return os;              // must return ostream&
    }
    // ...
    cout << "Home number: " << home << '\n';
    ```

---

[1] When inserting expressions, pay attention to the precedence of `<<`. Operators of lower precedence must be enclosed in parentheses.

[2] If it needs access to private data members, declare it to be a `friend`.

ostream& put(char)

- Writes a single character to a stream[1].

Examples:
```
cout.put( '\n' );          // same as cout << '\n';
cout.put( '!' ).put( bell );
```

ostream& write(const char* buf, int count)

ostream& write(
    const unsigned char* buf, int count
)

- Writes the specified number of characters pointed to by buf to a stream.

Example:
```
const int bufSize = 2048;
char buf[ bufSize ];
// ...
cout.write( buf, sizeof buf );
```

ostream& flush()

ostream& flush(ostream&)

- Forces buffered stream contents to be written. (The former is a member function; the latter is a manipulator.)

Examples:
```
cout << "What's your name? ";
cout.flush();
// ...
cout << "Where do you live? " << flush;
```

ostream& seekp(streampos, seek_dir=ios::beg)

- Moves the position of the "put" pointer in a file where streampos is an alias for an integral type and seek_dir specifies to what the position is relative: either the beginning, current position, or end of the file.

Example:
```
fileA.seekp( i * 100 );      // i'th block of 100
fileB.seekp( 100, ios::cur ); // forward 100 bytes
fileC.seekp( 0, ios::end );  // last character
```

---

1 Use of this over the << operator is dictated by user preference.

streampos tellp()

- Returns the current position of the "put" pointer in a file stream in bytes where `streampos` is an alias for an integral type.

  Example:
  ```
  streampos mark = myFile.tellp();
  ```

ostream& endl(ostream&)

- Inserts a `'\n'` and performs a `flush`.

  Example:
  ```
  cout << "Hello, world!" << endl;
  ```

Stream Input...

- Is achieved by using a variable of the `istream` or `iostream` class.

- Can be applied to the predefined input stream `cin` or to a user-defined input stream.

Extraction Operator...

- Reads a sequence of characters from the specified stream. Whitespace separates characters and is discarded[1].

- Is the >> operator overloaded.

- Is predefined for all simple types and pointer to `char`.

  Example:
  ```
  int age, weight;
  cout << "Enter age and weight: " << flush;
  cin >> age >> weight;   // read age, then weight
  ```

- Has the value of true so long as the end-of-file is not encountered (using the `operator void*()` conversion operator).

  Example:
  ```
  char c;
  while ( cin >> c )   // copy nonwhite cin to cout
      cout << c;
  ```

- Sets the `failbit` if the characters read from the stream are not of the appropriate type; sets the `badbit` if the read failed.

- Can be overloaded for `class` types in the same manner as the insertion operator (see "Insertion Operator" under "Stream Output").

---

[1] To read whitespace characters, use the member functions `get()`, `getline()`, or `read()`.

int get ( )

- Extracts and returns a single character from an input stream; whitespace is included.

- Has the value of EOF when the end-of-file is encountered[1]. (The failbit is never set.)

  Example:
  ```
  int c;
  while ( ( c = cin.get() ) != EOF )
      cout.put( c );
  ```

istream& get (char&)

istream& get (unsigned char&)

- Extracts a single character from an input stream; whitespace is included.

- Has the value of true so long as the end-of-file is not encountered.

  Example:
  ```
  char c;
  while ( cin.get( c ) )
      cout.put( c );
  ```

istream& get (char* buf, int limit, char delim = '\n')

istream& get (unsigned char* buf, int limit, char delim = '\n')

- Reads characters from a stream until either the delimiter is read, limit-1 characters are read (leaving space for the terminating null character), or until the end-of-file is encountered. The delimiter, if read, is *not* included in the character sequence and is left in the stream.

---

[1] The value of EOF must be distinct from all other characters; therefore, its value is generally -1. In the example, the variable c can not be declared to be a plain char since the implementation may equate char with unsigned char; therefore int is used.

```
istream& getline( char* buf,
   int limit, char delim = '\n'
)
istream& getline( unsigned char* buf,
   int limit, char delim = '\n'
)
```

- Reads characters from a stream until either the delimiter is read,
  `limit-1` characters are read (leaving space for the terminating
  null character), or until the end-of-file is encountered. The
  delimiter, if read, *is* included in the character sequence.

```
istream& read( char* buf, int count )
```

```
istream& read( unsigned char* buf, int count )
```

- Reads a string of characters from a stream.

  Example:
  ```
  const int bufSize = 2048;
  char buf[ bufSize ];
  // ...
  cin.read( buf, bufSize );
  ```

- Sets the `failbit` if the end-of-file is encountered before `count`
  characters have been read.

```
istream& ignore( int limit=1, int delim=EOF )
```

- Discards up to a specified number of characters or until a
  delimiter character is encountered from a stream.

```
int gcount()
```

- Returns the number of characters actually read by the last
  unformatted read operation on a stream.

```
istream& putback( char )
```

- Puts a character back onto a stream. At most, one character can
  be safely put back between successive calls to `get()`. The
  character should be the character that was obtained; the result is
  undefined otherwise.

```
int peek()
```

- Returns the next character awaiting to be read from a stream
  without actually reading it.

istream& seekg(streampos, seek_dir=ios::beg)

- Moves the position of the "get" pointer in a file where `streampos` is an alias for `long` and `seek_dir` specifies to what the position is relative: either the beginning, current position, or end of the file.

  Example:
  ```
  fileA.seekg( i * 100 );      // i'th block of 100
  fileB.seekg( 100, ios::cur ); // forward 100 bytes
  fileC.seekg( 0, ios::end );   // last character
  ```

streampos tellg()

- Returns the current position of the "get" pointer in a file stream in bytes.

  Example:
  ```
  streampos mark = myFile.tellg();
  ```

istream& ws(istream&)

- Extracts and discards whitespace characters from the specified stream.

  Example:
  ```
  cin >> ws;           // discard leading whitespace
  // ...
  ```

File Output...

- Is achieved by associating an output stream with a file using a variable of the `ofstream` or `fstream` class. These are defined in the `fstream.h` header file.

- Can be done just like regular stream output since the `ofstream` class is derived from the `ostream` class.

- Should be checked for failure.

  Example:
  ```
  ofstream outFile( "myFile" ); // try to open myFile
  if ( !outFile ) {              // open failed
     cerr << "cannot open \"myFile\" for output\n";
     exit( 1 );
  }
  outFile << "Wow!  This is even neater!\n";
  ```

- Has all existing data in the specified file discarded unless append mode is used. (See the values for the mode listed under "Open" under "Other File I/O.")

  Example:
  ```
  ofstream afterthought( "myFile", ios::app );
  afterthought << "On the other hand...\n";
  ```

File Input...

- Is achieved by associating an input stream with a file using a variable of the `ifstream` or `fstream` class. These are defined in the `fstream.h` header file.

- Can be used just like regular stream input since the `ifstream` class is derived from the `istream` class.

- Should be checked for failure.

  Example:
  ```
  ifstream inFile( "myFile" );  // try to open myFile
  if ( !inFile ) {              // open failed
     cerr << "cannot open \"myFile\" for input\n";
     exit( 1 );
  }
  int a, b;
  inFile >> a >> b;
  ```

Other File I/O

```
void open( char* name, int mode = ios::out,
   int prot = filebuf::openprot
   )
```

- Opens a file and associates it with a previously declared stream. The possible values for the mode are[1]:

ios::app	All data written is appended to the end of the file (implies ios::out).
ios::ate	All data written is appended to the end of the file (does not imply ios::out).
ios::in	The file is opened for input.
ios::out	The file is opened for output.
ios::trunc	Truncate (discard) the previous contents of the file (implied by ios::out).
ios::nocreate	If the file does not exist, the open() will fail.
ios::noreplace	If the file exists, the open() will fail.

- Establishes a protection mode prot[2].

```
void close()
```

- Closes a file and disassociates from a stream.

Example:
```
ifstream encyclopaedia;
// ...
for ( int i = 0; i < numVolumes; ++i ) {
   encyclopaedia.open( volume[ i ] );
   if ( !encyclopaedia )
      // handle failure to open
   // process file
   encyclopaedia.close();
}
```

---

[1] Modes may be combined with the bitwise-or operator.
[2] This is operating-system dependent.

Format States...

- Control the appearance of numbers when inserted into output streams and the format to extract numbers from input streams.

- Several flags control the formatting states; they can be changed using the `flags()`, `setf()`, and `unsetf()` member functions.

- Where noted, these bits comprise separate bit fields to be used with the `setf()` member function.

`skipws`	If set, skips whitespace on input for the extraction operator >>.
`left,` `right,` `internal`	Control the padding of a value using the fill character (see `fill()` below), either left- or right-justified, or internal[1].
	These three bits comprise the static member `ios::adjustfield`.
`dec, oct,` `hex`	Control the base used for insertion and extraction of integral types. If none are set, insertions default to decimal, but extractions are performed in the format of the integers: values with a leading 0 are taken to be octal, and values with a leading 0x or 0X are taken to be hexadecimal.
	These three bits comprise the static member `ios::basefield`.
`showbase`	If set, the base of integral values is output before the value: for octal, a leading 0, for hexadecimal, a 0x or 0X depending on the setting of the `uppercase` flag.
`showpoint`	If set, a decimal point and trailing zeros are output for floating-point numbers.
`showpos`	If set, a + will be inserted before output of a positive integral value.

---

[1] Right-justification is the default. When `internal` is specified, the fill character is added between any leading sign or base indication and the value.

scientific, fixed	If scientific is set, scientific notation is used for floating-point insertion[1].
	If fixed is set, a number of digits equal to the value set by precision() is inserted after the decimal point.
	If neither is set, the floating-point number will be inserted according to its value: scientific notation will be used if the exponent is less than -4 or greater than the current precision.
	These two bits comprise the static member ios::floatfield.
uppercase	If set, an uppercase X will be used for hexadecimal insertion if showbase is set, and an uppercase E will be used for floating-point insertion if scientific is set.

long flags()

• Returns the current format flags.

long flags(long)

• Sets the specified format flags and returns the previous flags.

Example:
```
long oldFlags = cout.flags();
// ...change some flags...
cout.flags( oldFlags );
```

long setf(long bitFlags)

• Turns on the specified format flags and returns the previous flags.

Example:
```
long oldFlags = cout.setf( ios::showbase );
```

---

[1] That is one digit, a decimal point, a number of digits equal to the value set by precision(), an e or an E depending on whether uppercase is set, and a signed exponent.

`long setf( long bitFlags, long bitField )`

- Clears the specified bit field then turns on the format flags and returns the previous flags[1].

- Must be used for bit flags belonging to either `ios::adjustfield, ios::basefield,` or `ios::floatfield.`

Example:
```
cout.setf( ios::scientific, ios::floatfield );
```

`long unsetf( long )`

- Turns off the specified format flags and returns the previous flags.

Example:
```
cout.unsetf( ios::showbase & ios::uppercase );
```

`ios& setiosflags( long )`

- Same as the `flags()` stream member function except that `setiosflags()` is a stream manipulator[2].

Example:
```
cout << setiosflags( ios::showpos );
```

`ios& resetiosflags( long )`

- Same as the `unsetf()` stream member function except that `resetiosflags()` is a stream manipulator[3].

Example:
```
cout << resetiosflags( ios::showpos );
```

`char fill( char )`

- Sets the "fill" character and returns the previous fill character. The default fill character is a space. (See `width()` below.)

---

[1] The important difference between this version of `setf()` and the former is that this one clears the bits of the bit field first. If the former were used in this example, it would turn on `ios::scientific` ignoring the possibility that `ios::fixed` might already be on; having both on doesn't make sense.

[2] To use `setioflags()`, `#include` the `<iomanip.h>` standard header file.

[3] To use `resetiosflags()`, `#include` the `<iomanip.h>` standard header file.

ostream& setfill(char)

- Same as the `fill()` stream member function except that `setfill()` is a stream manipulator[1].

char fill()

- Returns the current fill character.

int width(int minimum)

- Sets the minimum field-width to the given size and returns the previous field-width; zero means no minimum.

- When either the insertion or extraction stream operators are used and the value inserted or extracted is less than the field-width, then as many "fill" character are padded onto the value so as to make it equal to the minimum. If the value is equal to or greater than the field-width, nothing happens.

- The minimum field-width is reset to zero after each insertion or extraction.

int width()

- Returns the current minimum field-width.

ios& setw(int size)

- Prevents overflow of an input character vector by breaking up strings of characters that are larger than the specified buffer[2].

  Example:
  ```
  const int lineSize = 80;
  char line[ lineSize ];
  // ...
  while ( cin >> setw( lineSize ) >> line )
      // ...
  ```

---

[1] To use `setfill()`, `#include` the `<iomanip.h>` standard header file.
[2] To use `setw()`, `#include` the `<iomanip.h>` standard header file.

```
ios& dec( ios& )
ios& oct( ios& )
ios& hex( ios& )
ios& setbase( int )
```

- Changes the numerical base used to insert or extract integral types from a stream; setbase() is a stream manipulator[1].

   Example:
   ```
   int n = 1991;
   cout << "Decimal: " << n
   << oct << ", Octal: " << n
   << hex << ", Hexadecimal: " << n << endl;

   // when executed, produces...

   Decimal: 1991, Octal: 3707, Hexadecimal: 7c7
   ```

   Example:
   ```
   int d, o, h;
   cin >> d >> oct >> o >> hex >> h;
   ```

   Example:
   ```
   cout << setbase( 16 );
   ```

```
int precision( int )
```

- Sets the number of significant digits to be used when printing floating-point numbers and returns the previous value. The default is six digits.

```
ios& setprecision( int )
```

- Same as the precision() stream member function except that setprecision() is a stream manipulator[2].

```
int precision()
```

- Returns the current number of significant digits used to output floating-point numbers.

---

1 To use setbase(), #include the <iomanip.h> standard header file.
2 To use setprecision(), #include the <iomanip.h> standard header file.

Other Libraries

There are many C++ libraries (and C libraries ported to C++). A few of the common ones are listed here.

ctype.h...

- Provides macros for testing and manipulating characters in an implementation-independent way.

The following have the form: int *macro*(char c)

isalnum	c is a letter or decimal digit
isalpha	c is a letter
isascii	c is an ASCII character (code less than 128)
iscntrl	c is a control or delete (127) character
isdigit	c is a decimal digit
isgraph	c is a printing character other than a space
islower	c is a lower-case letter
isprint	c is a printing (non-control) character
ispunct	c is a punctuation character, that is, neither a control nor an alphanumeric character nor a space.
isspace	c is a whitespace character
isupper	c is an upper-case letter
isxdigit	c is a hexadecimal digit

The following have the form: char *macro*(char c)

toascii	convert integer to ASCII character
_tolower	convert upper-case character to lower-case
_toupper	convert lower-case character to upper-case
tolower	same as: (isupper(c) ? _tolower(c) : c)
toupper	same as: (islower(c) ? _toupper(c) : c)

---

string.h...

- Provides functions for handling strings, that is, null-terminated sequences of characters.

`int strlen( const char* s )`

- Returns the length of s, that is, the number of characters before the null-character.

  Example:
  ```
  char* message = "Hello world!";
  int length = strlen( message );   // length = 12
  ```

`char* strcpy( char* to, const char* from )`

`char* strncpy(`
`    char* to, const char* from , int limit`
`)`

- Copy to the address pointed to by to the string pointed to by from up to and including the null character; return to. The region pointed to by to must be large enough to hold the string.

- For strncpy(), at most limit characters are copied. The copied-to string is always null-terminated.

  Example:
  ```
  char* message = "You want it when?!";
  char buf[20];
  strcpy( buf, message );     // copy message to buf
  ```

`char* strcat( char* to, const char* from )`

`char* strncat(`
`    char* to, const char* from, int limit`
`)`

- Append a copy of the string pointed to by from to the end of the string pointed to by to; return to. The memory region pointed to by to must be large enough to hold the resultant string.

- For strncat(), at most limit characters are appended. The resultant string is always null-terminated.

  Example:
  ```
  char name[20] = "Humpty";
  strcat( name, " Dumpty" );     // append to name
  ```

```
int strcmp( const char* s1, const char* s2 )
int strncmp(
   const char* s1, const char* s2, int limit
)
```

- Lexicographically compare two strings. Returns -1, 0, or +1 if s1 is less than, equal to, or greater than s2, respectively.

- For strncmp(), at most limit characters are compared.

   Example:
   ```
   int index = 0, first = 0, last = N;
   while ( first <= last ) {
      index = ( first + last ) / 2;
      int result = strcmp( word, dictionary[index] );
      if ( result < 0 )
         last = index - 1;
      else if ( result > 0 )
         first = index + 1;
      else
         break;            // eureka!  we've found it!
   }
   ```

```
char* strchr( const char* s, char c )
char* strrchr( const char* s, char c )
```

- Search for the first occurrence of c in s; return pointer to character if c is in s, the null pointer otherwise.

- For strrchr(), (reverse) search for the last occurrence of c in s.

```
char* strpbrk(const char* s, const char* set)
```

- Searches for the first occurrence of any one of the characters in set in s; returns pointer to character if any one of the characters in set is in s, the null pointer otherwise.

```
int strspn( const char* s, const char* set )
int strcspn( const char* s, const char* set )
```

- Starting from the beginning of s, return the number of characters that are in set; stop when a character not in set is encountered.

- For strcspn(), returns the number of characters that are not in set; stops when a character in set is encountered.

Example:
```
char* s = "2000 North Naperville Road";
int n = strspn( s, "0123456789" );      // n = 4
```

```
char* strtok( const char* s, const char* set )
```

- Breaks strings into tokens using the characters in set as delimiters. Each time it is called, it returns a pointer to the start of a null-terminated token or the null pointer when there are no more tokens.

The first time strtok() is called for a string, it should be passed its address; for the second and subsequent times it is called, it should be passed the null pointer. This tells strtok() to continue to break up the same string.

When strtok() finds a token by finding a delimiter character, that character is overwritten in s with a null character to terminate the token[1]; between calls, strtok() saves a pointer to the succeeding character to continue on the next call.

Example:
```
void ToWords( register char* s ) {
    register char *word;
    while ( word = strtok( s, " " ) ) {
        cout << word << endl;
        s = 0;            // set to null to continue
    }
}
```

---

[1] So if you don't want the string to be modified, you have to copy it first.

limits.h...

- Provides implementation-dependent numerical constants. (The values listed are the minimum required by the ANSI standard.)

CHAR_BIT	8	number of bits in a byte
SCHAR_MIN	-127	min. value for signed char
SCHAR_MAX	+127	max. value for signed char
UCHAR_MAX	255	max. value for unsigned char
CHAR_MIN	0 or SCHAR_MAX	min. value of char
CHAR_MAX	UCHAR_MAX or SCHAR_MAX	max. value of char
MB_LEN_MAX	1	max. bytes in multibyte character
SHRT_MIN	-32767	min. value of short
SHRT_MAX	+32767	max. value of short
USHRT_MAX	65535	max. value of unsigned short
INT_MIN	-32767	min. value of int
INT_MAX	+32767	max. value of int
UINT_MAX	65535	max. value of unsigned int
LONG_MIN	-2147683647	min. value of long
LONG_MAX	+2147683647	max. value of long
ULONG_MAX	4294967295	max. value of unsigned long

math.h...

- Provides trigonometric and other mathematical functions.

  All trigonometric functions (`sin`, `cos`, etc.) use radians.

  Except where noted, each function takes one `double` argument; all functions return `double`.

`acos`	Arc-cosine.
`asin`	Arc-sine.
`atan`	Arc-tangent.
`atan2(y,x)`	Arc-tangent of `y`/`x`.
`ceil`	Ceiling.
`cos`	Cosine.
`cosh`	Hyperbolic cosine.
`exp`	Raise *e* to the power `x`.
`fabs`	Absolute value.
`floor`	Floor.
`fmod(x,y)`	Remainder of `x`/`y`.
`log`	Natural logarithm.
`log10`	Base-10 logarithm.
`pow(x,y)`	Raise `x` to the power `y`.
`sin`	Sine.
`sinh`	Hyperbolic sine.
`sqrt`	Square root.
`tan`	Tangent.
`tanh`	Hyperbolic tangent.

stdarg.h...

- Provides a mechanism for writing functions that take a varying number of arguments of an unspecified type.

- Defines three macros for this purpose:

```
void  va_start( va_list, last-argument )
type  va_arg( va_list, type )
void  va_end( va_list )
```

va_start initializes the argument list where *last-argument* is the last one specified in the declaration.

va_arg retrieves the next argument from the argument list of the specified type.

va_end cleans up the argument list.

Example:

```
void NumPrint( const char* format ... ) {
    va_list arg;
    va_start( arg, format );    // init arg pointer

    for ( char* p = format; *p; ++p )
        if ( *p == '%' )
            switch ( *++p ) {
            case 'd':
                int ival = va_arg( arg, int );
                cout << ival;
                break;
            case 'f':
                double dval = va_arg( arg, double );
                cout << dval;
                break;
            }
        else
            cout << *p;

    va_end( arg );              // clean up
}
```

stdlib.h...

- Provides several assorted functions for various tasks including program termination and numerical conversion.

void exit(int)

- Causes program termination[1].

- Returns a status code to the program's environment[2].

- Calls all destructors for class objects that have static storage class.

void abort()

- Causes immediate program termination[3].

- Typically causes an additional, implementation-dependent action[4].

int atoi(char*)

- Converts a string to an integer.

long atol(char*)

- Converts a string to a long integer.

double atof(char*)

- Converts a string to a double.

---

1 A `return` statement in the function `main()` is equivalent to calling `exit()` with the return value as its argument.
2 The use of and values for such status codes are implementation dependent, although zero usually means that the program executed successfully and any non-zero value indicates an error.
3 That is, unlike `exit()`, it does not call destructors.
4 An example would be where the contents of memory are saved to disk allowing a postmortem to be performed on a program.

ASCII Character Set

Below is a table of the ASCII character set with the values for each character listed in decimal, octal, and hexadecimal. For the control characters, that is, those with codes less than 32 decimal, the mnemonic and meaning are also listed. (A "^" means that the control key is used in conjunction with the letter following it.)

Dec	Oct	Hex	Key	Mnem	Meaning
0	000	00	^@	NUL	Null
1	001	01	^A	SOH	Start of Heading
2	002	02	^B	STX	Start of Text
3	003	03	^C	ETX	End of Text
4	004	04	^D	EOT	End of Transmission
5	005	05	^E	ENQ	Enquiry
6	006	06	^F	ACK	Acknowledge
7	007	07	^G	BEL	Bell
8	010	08	^H	BS	Backspace
9	011	09	^I	HT	Horizontal Tab
10	012	0A	^J	LF	Linefeed (Newline)
11	013	0B	^K	VT	Vertical Tab
12	014	0C	^L	FF	Form Feed
13	015	0D	^M	CR	Carriage Return
14	016	0E	^N	SO	Shift Out
15	017	0F	^O	SI	Shift In
16	020	10	^P	DLE	Data Link Escape
17	021	11	^Q	DC1	Device Control 1
18	022	12	^R	DC2	Device Control 2
19	023	13	^S	DC3	Device Control 3
20	024	14	^T	DC4	Device Control 4
21	025	15	^U	NAK	Negative Acknowledgment
22	026	16	^V	SYN	Synchronous Idle
23	027	17	^W	ETB	End of Transmission Block
24	030	18	^X	CAN	Cancel
25	031	19	^Y	EM	End of Medium
26	032	1A	^Z	SUB	Substitute
27	033	1B	^[	ESC	Escape
28	034	1C	^\	FS	File Separator
29	035	1D	^]	GS	Group Separator
30	036	1E	^^	RS	Record Separator
31	037	1F	^_	US	Unit Separator

Dec	Oct	Hex	Key	Dec	Oct	Hex	Key
32	040	20	(space)	80	120	50	P
33	041	21	!	81	121	51	Q
34	042	22	"	82	122	52	R
35	043	23	#	83	123	53	S
36	044	24	$	84	124	54	T
37	045	25	%	85	125	55	U
38	046	26	&	86	126	56	V
39	047	27	'	87	127	57	W
40	050	28	(	88	130	58	X
41	051	29	)	89	131	59	Y
42	052	2A	*	90	132	5A	Z
43	053	2B	+	91	133	5B	[
44	054	2C	,	92	134	5C	\
45	055	2D	-	93	135	5D	]
46	056	2E	.	94	136	5E	^
47	057	2F	/	95	137	5F	_
48	060	30	0	96	140	60	`
49	061	31	1	97	141	61	a
50	062	32	2	98	142	62	b
51	063	33	3	99	143	63	c
52	064	34	4	100	144	64	d
53	065	35	5	101	145	65	e
54	066	36	6	102	146	66	f
55	067	37	7	103	147	67	g
56	070	38	8	104	150	68	h
57	071	39	9	105	151	69	i
58	072	3A	:	106	152	6A	j
59	073	3B	;	107	153	6B	k
60	074	3C	<	108	154	6C	l
61	075	3D	=	109	155	6D	m
62	076	3E	>	110	156	6E	n
63	077	3F	?	111	157	6F	o
64	100	40	@	112	160	70	p
65	101	41	A	113	161	71	q
66	102	42	B	114	162	72	r
67	103	43	C	115	163	73	s
68	104	44	D	116	164	74	t
69	105	45	E	117	165	75	u
70	106	46	F	118	166	76	v
71	107	47	G	119	167	77	w
72	110	48	H	120	170	78	x
73	111	49	I	121	171	79	y
74	112	4A	J	122	172	7A	z
75	113	4B	K	123	173	7B	{
76	114	4C	L	124	174	7C		
77	115	4D	M	125	175	7D	}
78	116	4E	N	126	176	7E	~
79	117	4F	O	127	177	7F	DEL

Index